EX-PASTORS

EX-PASTORS

Why Men Leave the Parish Ministry

Gerald J. Jud, Ph.D.
Edgar W. Mills, Jr., Ph.D.
Genevieve Walters Burch, M.A.

PILGRIM PRESS
Philadelphia · Boston

CONTENTS

PREFACE

A close friend sent the newspaper clipping. I read it with great interest and concern because it was about another friend. However, except for the name, the story is familiar. It points to a phenomenon of our time. Here is the story in its entirety:

MINISTER CAN'T PLAY THE ROLE

Fifteen years ago, . . . entered the ministry, dedicated to the ideal of touching the world through the arms of the church.

Yesterday, discouraged and heartsick, . . . announced his resignation from the pulpit of St. Paul's United Church of Christ, where he has been pastor since 1962.

In a letter to his congregation, . . . said, "It simply has become too clear to be any longer ignored, that my understanding of mature religious faith, and my understanding of the role of the church and its ministry, are almost totally at variance with the views of the vast majority of the organized church.

"My commitment," said . . . , "is to an ideal about life and its meaning. The commitment of the church, if at all, is to a body of doctrines or to the institution of the church and its preservation at all costs, and only very incidentally to any kind of social concern. I could conform (or pretend to conform) my views to the expectations of the institutionalized church, or I could leave the professional ministry. I have chosen the latter course as the most honest, and fairest to the church and my own integrity."

. . . will move to Northfield and go into a retailing partnership there when his resignation takes effect in mid-September, he said.

"It just became intolerable to me," he said today. "I couldn't live with myself any longer."

Why did . . . go into the ministry at all? "Originally my motivation was to make the ministry more relevant. But you can't fight the role. At any rate, I discovered that I couldn't."

"The church is looking to the past," he said. "It is primarily concerned with theological crap and not at all concerned with life."

This book is about ex-pastors, those men who have left the pastoral ministry to earn their living outside the church as institution. It is a disciplined attempt to learn from them and about them in the hopes that what we hear and learn might affect the policy and the shape of the church in our time.

In recent years the Board for Homeland Ministries of the United Church of Christ has been holding theme conferences at its conference grounds in Deering, New Hampshire. These conferences built around some pressing question bring together church professionals as peers to pool their expertise and learn from one another. In October 1967 Howard Spragg, now executive vice-president of the UCC Board for Homeland Ministries, proposed that we invite the persons in the UCC who have dropped out of the parish ministry. The suggestion appeared to be a good one and plans were set in motion for the conference.

A little investigation, however, showed what we should all have known. These men now employed in business, industry, colleges and universities, and in service organizations could not easily take off two weeks for a conference. An alternative plan would have to be found.

On December 28, 1967 a group of persons with specialized interest in the field met at the National Council of Churches in New York City. Gerald J. Jud, who had been given the assignment for the conference, extended the invitation to the "Think Tank" saying, "The UCC Board for Homeland Ministries has a concern to do disciplined listening to persons who have left the pastoral ministry to earn their living from other sources than the church. Your counsel concerning ways of procedure is much needed."

At the meeting the following persons were present: Howard E. Spragg, executive vice-president of the United Church Board for Homeland Ministries; Earl D. C. Brewer, executive director of research of the National Council of Churches; Edgar W. Mills, Jr., director of the NCC Ministry Studies Board; Jack C. Biersdorf, executive director, NCC Department of Ministry; Henry Adams, then staff member of the NCC Department of Ministry, now executive director, Academy of Parish Clergy; Father Gerard Waldorf, S.J., counselor at "Bearings," 229 East 79th Street, New York City; Harold Wilke, executive director of the UCC Council for Church and Ministry; George Nishimoto, staff member of the UCC Council for Church and Ministry; Willis E. Elliott, staff member of the UCC Division of Evangelism; Gerald J. Jud, general secretary of the UCC Division of Evangelism; John Snook, professor of religion at Barnard College; W. Ebert Hobbs, executive director of the NCC Department of Church Renewal; Thomas Wieser, staff member of the NCC Department of Church Renewal; Frank White, staff member of the NCC Department of Church Renewal.

The meeting turned out to be an exciting event. A consensus emerged noting that not only had many men left the pastoral ministry but in all churches many others were wrestling through the decision to leave. But too little is known about this phenomenon and about these men. Not only is little known but many church administrators have looked upon these men as traitors or as enemies of the church. So the wisdom of the ex-pastors was not being tapped. There had obviously been an institutional failure in listening to and in ministering to these men.

Out of our mutual concern and interest that day a coalition was formed to pool our expertise and interest in behalf of the ministry and the research now plainly needed. Some agreements were reached.

United Church Board for Homeland Ministries would (1) press its primary concern: to do disciplined listening to the ex-pastors so that the ex-pastors might inform the work of the church; (2) express caring for them; (3) provide funds for the necessary conferences and research; (4) seek to model a style of research tied in to the NCC Departments of Research and Ministry, and then share its data with policy-makers in other denominations in the hopes that when they do research they will tie in to the NCC research team (thus assuring validity) and share their data with us.

The NCC Department of Research, through its head, Dr. Brewer, agreed to the above concept and offered its services with a whole heart. Dr. Biersdorf of the Department of Ministry and Dr. Mills of the Ministry Studies Board expressed great interest in their Careers Studies Research and agreed that this ministry and research could be seen within the context of that research. Dr. Wilke and his staff would have responsibility to use the data emerging in the strengthening of their work among ministers in the United Church of Christ.

I was given oversight relative to the UCC research project, reporting to Dr. Spragg. It became my responsibility to ready data and interpretation for publication and distribution. Dr. Mills agreed to head the research from the perspective of the Career Patterns Study. Dr. Brewer (who has since returned to his teaching post at the Candler School of Theology, Emory University) agreed to work closely with us, especially in the development of necessary research instruments and in the early tabulation of data.

A very important addition to our team was made when we learned that Mrs. Hobart (Genevieve) Burch, a Ph.D. candidate at the University of Maryland, was also doing work in the very field we wanted to investigate. Thus we had the benefit of her disciplined and scholarly mind almost from the beginning of the study.

In order to get at our task we agreed on the following methods: (a) to hold four conferences to which, on a regional basis, all the known men in the UCC who have withdrawn from the pastoral ministry would be invited; (b) to devise research instruments to learn from and about these ex-pastors; (c) to report our findings to church policy-makers.

This book is now a reporting of what was learned from these men and about them, the advice they have for the church and its related institutions, and at last the policy implications for the church arising from this study.

Here in focus is a most important group of people. As part of the life and history of the church they have given much and have much to give. They are a mixture, as all of us are, of strengths and weaknesses, of wisdom and folly. They need our love and concern, and we need what they have to give. If we fail to relate to them, if we fail to include them as important partners in the dialogue in the church, if we fail to let them inform the policy of the church, we will do so at our peril.

The authors of this book worked closely together throughout the study. Although some aspects of our collaboration were as delicate as the mating dance of the whooping crane, we survived and we have our friendship and this book to prove it. Whereas the three of us are responsible for the entire contents of the report, we did divide the work of final writing. Edgar Mills wrote chapters 2, 3, and 5; Genevieve Burch wrote chapter 4; I wrote chapters 1 and 6. Genevieve Burch is also responsible for much of the computer work. The instruments used to gather the data are given in Appendix A; the tabulation of the results appears in Appendix B.

The computer time for this study was made available through the facilities of the Computer Science Center of the University of Maryland.

GERALD J. JUD

INTRODUCTION

It is a pleasure to be associated with this research project and to write this brief introduction. It is not, however, an easy task to write about the book. It contains confessional statements from ex-pastors, statistical summaries of responses, theoretical interpretations by the researchers, and policy implications of the study set forth by a denominational executive deeply concerned about the local church in a new time. These disparate pieces and approaches tend to unify around the malaise of the churches. Indeed, the book explores one of the symptoms of our spiritual sickness with the hope that out of diagnosis may come prescription.

The United Church of Christ is to be congratulated for initiating an inquiry into the sensitive question of why pastors are leaving ecclesiastical employment. Focused upon the situation in one denomination, the project was carried out under ecumenical auspices, and its results should be useful to leaders of various denominations. It is my understanding that the results of this study will be shared with all the policy-makers in American Protestantism and that a concerted attempt will be made to take initiatives across denominational lines in order to address the trouble in the system of the church. In this case a denomination has underwritten the cost of research relative to a serious problem we all have. It is to be hoped that other denominations will follow this model, share their learnings, and develop initiative in the same way. In this period of rapid change careful research should inform policy development. Since denominations share many problems in common, the model of research here demonstrated will get the research done, paid for, and properly used.

Although considerable publicity has centered around certain cases, it is difficult to determine the level or the trends in the rates of persons leaving ecclesiastical employment. The rates are doubtless lower than for occupational changes generally. Yet the common practice is to ordain a clergyman for life, and any defection from ordination vows or clerical employment is felt to be more serious than an ordinary change of occupation. Thus, church leaders would do well to listen to ex-pastors and to learn the circumstances surrounding their decisions to quit. This report provides such an opportunity.

The focus of this study has been upon the clergy. Often the laity has "taken a beating" as causative in the "tipping point" precipitating discontinuance of pastoral employment. Lay leaders need to be heard from on this issue. The results of this study should be reviewed by lay leaders in the denominations and in congregations. Then, opportunities should be given for the laymen to speak! If the laity is as much of a problem as indicated in various sections of this report, and if the missionary congregation is dependent upon the development of a new breed of laity, obviously more lay leadership should appear in bureaucracies of denominations and in the leadership of such efforts.

The theoretical underpinning for this project has been drawn, in somewhat eclectic fashion, from studies in the fields of careers, occupations, and professions. The applicability of this approach to the clergy as calling, mission, and ministry needs to be explored. Indeed, the occupation of pastor and the calling to mission may be very different. At least it seemed so to many ex-pastors and doubtless would appear so to many more laymen. In any case, it would be interesting to construct typical points in the life cycle of ministry as career and as mission. This would call for theoretical elaboration both by social scientists and theologians and for research among both clergy and laity.

The complaints about the inadequacies of theological education are old and likely to continue. This hoary, outdated, and conservative style of education has been little touched by recent student rebellions. Yet there should be increased outside as well as inside pressure upon theological schools to update their educational practices. Even if such pressures were moderately successful, however, the changes in the society are so great that constant and continuous retraining opportunities for clergy and laity must be found. The timing and content of such retraining could be considerably informed by the findings of this study.

This project points to greater attention to the conditions under which clergymen are called upon to serve, such as income levels, working arrangements, changes from church to church, challenging situations for ministry and mission, and so on. Of course, closely related are the conceptions of the laity regarding these conditions. Also, they involve the "small church syndrome" in view of the large number of very small parishes in most Protestant denominations. Clusters of congregations could ecumenically and locally work toward solutions of some of these issues.

Although this project explored only a tiny segment of church life today, it has touched a raw nerve which is causing pain and anguish at many points in the modern system of denominational Christianity. Implications of the results should be practically pursued along many fronts, including congregations, theological education, laity, theological developments, personnel practices, church bureaucracies, life cycle, and surrounding support patterns for the ministry as an occupation.

If taken seriously, any one of these, or several in various combinations, could become entry points for responsible change-agents to perform needed surgery on the church body to bring it closer to being the body of Christ and doing his bidding in the world.

This would doubtless involve modern systems analysis, as suggested in the final chapter. It would call for the enmeshment of many parts into a larger whole. Such parts would need to include the life cycle of the individual (lay and clergy), the career cycle of the clergy with emphasis on stress points, the church as a system (congregation, theological school, administrative and programming bureaucracies, etc.), and various elements of the sociocultural environment. With a focus on the interpenetrative life and career cycles, systems analysis would involve open relationships to all other relevant parts and pressures in an input-output model focused on goal-seeking behavior with feedback evaluation and modification of action. Indeed, the challenge to follow up this project with such a systems analysis of the church—its laity and clergy—in contemporary, changing society, if actually carried out, theoretically and practically, could become one of its most important results.

Meantime, back in the congregations, in the homes of laity and clergy, in bureaucracies of all denominations, in ecumenical circles, and in theological schools, this research report should be read and discussed. It could become the basis for individual and corporate decisions and actions in the modern mission of the Christian church.

EARL D. C. BREWER
Professor of Sociology and Religion
Candler School of Theology, Emory University
Atlanta, Georgia

1 / COUNSEL FROM THE EX–PASTORS

This project began with the intention of doing disciplined listening to persons who have left the pastoral ministry to earn their living from sources other than the church.

We were inclined to listen. We wanted to learn from them and to find ways whereby their witness could inform the life of the church. This book is a report of what we have learned about this group of men, and we hope that our reporting is a sign of our listening to them.

This chapter begins the report of what we have learned. Specifically it is a report of data gotten from Part I of the questionnaire mailed to clergy in nonecclesial employment (see Appendix A) and from Part V of the questionnaire given to the control groups of pastors (see Appendix A).

In this questionnaire we asked for counsel in the following manner:

> From your experience in leaving ministerial work, what suggestions would you like to make to each of the following (use extra pages as needed):
>
> 1. The congregation (or other religious organization) whose employ you most recently left?
> 2. Your seminary?
> 3. Fellow pastors?
> 4. Laymen?
> 5. Church administrators (conference, association, national staff)?

The Response of Ex-Pastors

The response was exceedingly good. Out of the 370 persons on our list, 241 responded. Among the pastors 276 responded. Many of them used extra pages and still others sent special papers which they had prepared. The material is too voluminous to report here. However, the material has been read with great care several times and the authors will seek to be faithful to the spirit of the material.

1

Insofar as possible the counsel will be presented in the words of the correspondents. Their words bear the marks of authenticity, coming as they do from the hot crucible of suffering, anger, pain, and vision.

It is important to remember that this group of persons is in no sense monolithic. In fact, it is extremely varied and there is sometimes strong disagreement. This chapter does not attempt to present advice as though it were from a single person but as coming from different persons with different experience and different perspectives. One man has found his faith radically changed, another is full of anger, another is full of pain, and still another has found that a greater vision has replaced his former one and though he still loves and supports the church, he is following a larger vision. Still others write in strong affectional terms concerning the church. Here, in their own words, is the witness of different moods of our respondents.

CHANGE IN FAITH

While I admit to occasional feelings of anger and disappointment toward each of the groups listed here, I cannot, in truth, blame them or criticize them for the changes in my faith which led me to leave the pastorate. I left when my prayers were meaningless literary productions, when hymns only evoked a comfortable nostalgia, when my sermons could not say what I felt, when the Bible became literature, when missions and social actions became philanthropy and civil rights, when Jesus became a man, and when God died on my lips.

• • •

It would be somewhat absurd for me to offer advice—and perhaps somewhat dangerous—for I am not very sure that I could believe tomorrow what was said today. Perhaps I would most likely tell the church to go off to be religious if it wants to, but to please leave Jesus the Christ out of things—leave him to those who mourn him dead, who celebrate him victorious, and who follow him voluntarily. Perhaps I would say, "Stop trying to point out the true way to faith. You don't really have it—none do. If it was ever really known or knowable, it somehow got lost way back when." Perhaps I would say to individuals, "Stop worrying about the true faith, whether you've got the correct doctrine, whether the communion should include wine, whether the church needs new stained-glass windows, or whether the choir can sing on key. Try—just try—to let yourself do a little good, not a lot, just a little."

ANGER

Drop dead.

• • •

My first inclination is to say, "Go to hell!" but more reflection dictates that would be neither theologically sound nor practical. Actually there is a small concerned group left in the congregation—numbering perhaps three—and if I had any counsel for them it would be to get out—resign and become active in the Democratic Party, the League of Women Voters, the Poverty Program, or . . .

PAIN

These are the briefest of answers. Orally I would expand but it really tears me apart to sit and write, only. For my own psychological health much of the brutality I met in the church has been submerged, to be brought up again only in the presence of another warm human being who stands with me. The mere typing of these brief words brings tears.

GREATER VISION

In one particular fashion we all became involved in battling for an unpopular ordinance on the ballot, although my own church people were largely against it.

That was when I saw the need for a new evangel, the good news that men of goodwill gathered in tiny clusters for mutual forgiveness and learning, and actions *can* penetrate the "old society" of secure institutions and save them from their deadness and doom.

I wanted to make this thing grow. More than anything else I wanted to awaken "new men" to recognize each other and to devote themselves to the task of being the "new society" now.

• • •

I dropped out of the parish ministry—with the encouragement of my wife who wanted to pick up her interrupted career as a social worker. I became a writer—the dream I shelved when I married her and entered seminary. I launched half a dozen manuscripts aimed at the new evangel: a novel, plays, short stories, articles.

• • •

Dropped out? No, I dived in.

TWO DIFFERENT WORLDS

I really have no suggestions for the groups of people or institutions listed below. It seems that my own religious orientation is poles apart from that of most other individuals, groups, or institutions. I find the gulf cannot really be bridged; and for the moment, at least, I have given up any serious attempts at even trying.

To state the schism briefly and simply, most religious people seem to feel some sort of positive passion and loyalty toward the physical institutional church. They find some sort of strength and power residing in the confines of the local, regional, national, or universal church. Some find it at one level, others find it at other levels, but they are "turned on" at least one step or another. As I search through the corridors of the institutional church, I find only an emotional and spiritual void. What spiritual strength and power I possess, if indeed I possess any, seems to come from the roots of my own existence, or from other lonely like-minded individuals who share my religious experience.

Since such a position is either incomprehensible or relegated to the realm of neurosis by most people, it is a futile task indeed to offer either suggestions or criticism of any nature. Not only that, but *we are struggling in two different worlds,* and what appears relevant in one is irrelevant in the other and vice versa.

AFFECTIONAL TERMS

Some of the men wrote in strong affectional terms. They are not leaving the ministry to a local church because they have been hurt by the people or the institution, or because they are no longer hopeful about it; they simply have caught a greater vision and are following it. They want to stay in close relation and want to be considered Christian ministers. Thus:

> Many of you have spoken many times of how I have helped you. I am glad that you feel that way, though I sometimes think you have given me more credit than I deserve. I wish I could convey to you somehow a measure of how much your love and loyalty to the cause of Christ has meant to me, and given me satisfaction and encouragement. As I move into a different field of endeavor, I hope you will continue to think of me as a minister. For a minister is not simply one who seeks to preach and teach the word of God in a formal church situation; he is one who seeks to express the love of God in each human relationship every day in all of life's arena. As I ask you to continue to think of me as a minister, so would I ask you to think of yourselves as ministers in the very same way. God needs ministers—lots of them: merchant ministers, housewife ministers, parent ministers, farm ministers, mechanic ministers, student ministers, and a multitude of others.

Ex-Pastors' Advice to the Congregation

If you fear *change,* both personal and social; if you demand twelfth-century theology and Christianity from your ministers; if you feel that the Christian faith is something to be locked up within the four walls of a church building; if you feel it just and fair to hire a man and his wife—who have together put in approximately 12 to 15 years of study and training for required degrees—to work for you, to be religious for you on a full-time basis for the part-time salary of one unskilled, untrained, and uneducated individual; if you feel that it is a Christian virtue—preparing one for sainthood—to allow one's self and family to be exploited physically, emotionally, spiritually, and financially; *then you are probably a typical and average American congregation calling yourself the body of Christ.*

My recommendation is that you give up the phoney church image, put away your pious platitudes, your saccharin sentimentalism of the nineteenth century, blow out the candles of your churches, lock the doors of your neo-Gothic buildings, and go home and forget the whole thing and become *real people.*

There is a lot of feeling in that passage, a lot of anger and a lot of pain, a lot of disappointment, and a strong feeling of having been exploited. The love of the church is there, but it is not so much a love of the church as the church is, as what the church may become. Moreover there is a strong feeling here concerning a lack of reality in the church, and the implication that those who are outside the church are more real than those who are inside. It is an excellent summary both in idea and feeling tone. The feelings contained here are expressed through the reporting of the many ex-pastors in this study.

The issues pointed to in the passage are: 1. The world has changed. The church has not. Join the twentieth century. In order to do this the Christian faith needs to be relevant to the times and related to the needs of men out in the world. The church is turned in on itself, too much shut away from human need and the great issues that demand the attention of modern man. 2. I have been exploited by a church which has poor personnel policies and which has failed to understand aright the role of the Christian pastor.

Get with the Changed World

There is little doubt that most of these men who have opted out of the pastoral ministry are men who have allowed the radical changes of this world, and the radical difference of this age, to penetrate their conscious life. They have borne the pain of experiencing the obsolescence of many of the old church forms and have lost their patience; they have simply not been able to wait while the local church makes its tortuous and glacially slow moves toward the future.

These men are not only aware that the world has changed and that to be faithful the church must speak in contemporary idiom, but *they feel also that the deeds of the church must be deeds which address the plight of man in this revolutionary world* and that the institutional concerns are not the prime business of the church. Says one man:

> I have felt more freedom to express myself politically since leaving the pastorate. I hope you have grown to see that the business of the church is to bear a moral witness in the arena of public decision-making, and that the business of the church is to be identified more closely with the plight of the unrepresented and the dispossessed. My present involvement in social work permits me to be more constructively and personally related to such people than I could be when leading worship was my primary role expectation.

Another one says:

> I would suggest that the concerns of God's world are of infinitely more importance than the institutional concerns of the church; that whether starving children get fed in South America is much more urgent than how many turkeys to order for the "fellowship dinner"; that whether we con-

tinue killing people in Vietnam is of more consequence than whether we can pick up a tenor for the choir; that whether there is going to be reconciliation between black and white is more important than whether we need wall-to-wall carpeting in the chancel.

And yet another one:

In the corporate life of the church as in personal life it is profoundly true that "whoever would save his life will lose it and whoever loses his life for my sake will find it." If we are to be where Christ is to be found and if we are to be faithful to our servant role in the world, everything the church holds dear must be seen as expendable. The church school, the sacred day (Sunday), the sacred place (building), the sacred guy (minister), preaching, choir—everything we have associated with the church in the past—we must be prepared to give up in the new day. The church primarily concerned with institutional maintenance and self-preservation is not worth trying to save. It is already dead.

PERSONNEL POLICIES

Have a definite *job description* for the minister.

* * *

Treat him as a leader—not a handmaid.

* * *

Allow the minister to lead a life separate from church if he so desires.

* * *

A man's home is his *privacy*. Do not regulate this life.

* * *

Congregations ought to at least *meet minimum personnel policies* and practices adhered to in the business world, in treatment of their professional leadership.

* * *

Somehow local congregations must begin to do their business as institutions. This means that the *lines of authority* must be clarified so that the minister is responsible to the board and not to every member of the congregation. This means that the minister must be paid as a professional.

* * *

Accept your pastor *as a person* rather than as a thing to be bought, manipulated, and exploited. Let him have a beer if he wants to. PK's have a hell of a time in our society.

* * *

Accept the minister as a human being with strengths and weaknesses but not as a superhuman person; and second, I would suggest that they show the pastor that his efforts are appreciated.

* * *

Pay the pastor a salary commensurate with his profession [mentioned over and over again] and training.

. . .

Show appreciation for a man's work.

Here the men make an indictment of the poor practices of many local churches relative to personnel. The advice to every church seems to be: Your practices relative to your professional leadership are very poor. You can improve the situation by:

1. Having a clear job description for your pastor.

> The activities and role expectations of the "typical clergyman" are out-of-date and/or out-of-touch with current needs. One implication of this fact is that the ministry tends to dehumanize weak men who enter it, and repel strong men who consider it.
>
> Generally, I feel that the response to modern human needs of both clergymen and congregations is not one which reflects the freeing message of the gospel. These forms are tradition and structure bound beyond all theological justification. The living Spirit of God is free in the world, while everywhere the "churchmen" seem to be limited in their response by chains of their own creation. For the man who would seek to be part of the new worldly responsiveness, it is clearly preferable not to depend on the archaic structures for both guidance and livelihood.

2. Allowing your pastor to have a private life.

> Have a greater awareness of the stresses and strains on the parsonage family. A realization that though the minister is set apart he is also human, with similar needs of friends, social interaction.

3. Clarifying lines of authority in the church.

> Somehow local congregations must begin to do their business as institutions. This means that the lines of authority must be clarified so that the minister is responsible to the board and not to every member of the congregation. This means that the minister must be seen as a knowledgeable professional who has been hired to do a job which calls for specific skills. This means that he must be paid as a professional.

4. Treating your pastor as a professional but also as a person who has the same rights and needs you have to be loved, to be angry, to be hurt and full of pain and afraid.

5. Paying him a decent salary.

> Though I do not "blame" the local parish (though my last five years were very unhappy ones) I do feel that the internal institutional concerns do dominate too much of the time and energy of the active members. Further, they tend to be too critical of the pastor and uncritical of them-

selves. Tradition is "worshiped" and innovation or new directions are discouraged if not eliminated. Also the minister's wife and family have unfair demands placed upon them (both by the minister and the congregation). Little concern is shown over the economic stress on the minister and if he raises the issue, some feel he is "unchristian" or unmotivated. I am happy to be out of the parish trap.

IMPROVE PLANNING IN THE CHURCH

The contemporaneity of these men is indicated by their frequent mentioning that the local church should cop to good *planning* if it is to join the twentieth century. There is throughout their testimony an underlying assumption that the church does not plan adequately, that it is unclear about goals and objectives and that it is weak also in the strategy department—that is, in translating the goals it has into clearcut strategies.

> Take a good objective look at yourselves in terms of what you really are accomplishing for your members, the community, and the outside world as against the cost in money, time, and energy expended in the church program. Just what are you trying to accomplish, merely keeping a traditional, time-honored institution alive?
> Define your goals more realistically. Go after the goals as redefined.
>
> • • •
>
> *Develop criteria and methods for periodic review* and evaluation of (1) specific congregational goals and emphases, and (2) the effectiveness of your pastor in fulfilling his role in reference to the accepted goals and emphases. Develop ways of communicating official appreciation for services rendered. Find out ways of hammering out congregational priorities together with the pastor so that the pastor and official board are working as a team in pursuing the accepted goals.
>
> • • •
>
> The congregation needs to get straight on what its purposes are, and to adjust its priorities accordingly. If they are to continue as a pleasant low-key social fellowship and status-bestowing agency, for everyone's peace of mind they ought to seek leadership without awareness of or conscience about social issues. If (as some wish) they are to understand themselves as a group with some genuine mission to fulfill in the world, they must find a way to cut down their narcissistic spending on property, and fund service programs much more adequately.

FACE CONFLICT CREATIVELY

These men know the experiencing of conflict. Since the world has changed radically, they are aware that the church cannot live without conflict. They are not unaware that they have serious conflicts in their own being but they plead with the church to face conflict openly and not to run away from it. Because the local church generally runs from conflict, *dishonesty about feelings and ideas is often rampant* and this makes it difficult to join the twentieth century. The need to see conflict as a given, as an opportunity for growth and development, for the clarification of issues and goals, and even for the discernment of the gospel, is seen by these men.

> I believe congregations need to struggle more openly and honestly with controversy and with controversial issues, for they are the ones that count. That is to say, I have not found much enthusiasm for Paul's admonition to speak the truth in love. Too often the love is superficial and the truth is somewhere else.

Pastors' Advice to the Local Church

There is really not much difference in the reporting of the ex-pastors and the pastors, though on a feeling level the ex-pastors are one step more intense. The ex-pastors tend to be angrier and less hopeful about the local church as a viable institution. However, this is only a matter of degree. And it would be a gross error to infer that the pastors are not angry and in considerable pain. They have very strong feelings about where the church is in terms of the new age, and show an impatience only a few steps away from the ex-pastors. They say:

> Wake up, get with it!
>
> • • •
>
> Give up outmoded ways of thinking.
>
> • • •
>
> Fish or cut bait!
>
> • • •
>
> Get in or get out! [This theme occurs very often.]
>
> • • •
>
> Stop thinking that the old-time religion began in the 1800's.

The pastors urge their congregations to quit emphasizing tradition so much. They call upon them to be more relevant and more open.

Since the pastors are still in the system there is much stronger emphasis on salary inequities, housing and employment practices. Many wrote in detail relative to these matters.

The ex-pastors seldom mentioned worship. It was mentioned much more frequently by the pastors, but when they mentioned it they did so in terms of pointing out the obsolescence of present forms and they urged change.

The pastors not only show more hope for the institutional local church but they do so together with imaginative reporting of exciting new things happening. They mention theology more often, though sometimes it is in a platitudinous form.

The pastors plead with congregations to quit being suspicious of the pastor and give him better support. Many urge, too, that appreciation goes a long way.

Pastors mention often that the church is a community, not a building, and that persons are more important than buildings.

Anyone reading the material sent by the correspondent pastors would surely be struck by the similarity of the reporting of the ex-pastors and the pastors. For those who want updating in the church, there is much reason to take heart here. For those who want the church primarily rooted in the past, there is good reason to tremble.

Ex-Pastors' Counsel to Laymen

It is difficult to extricate advice to laymen from the foregoing advice to local churches. But this advice was asked of them, and some "picture in the head" emerges when we look at what the ex-pastors said to the laymen.

UNDERSTANDING THE ROLE OF THE PASTOR

"Get a better understanding of the role of the pastor." This counsel appeared far more often than any other, indicating again the ex-pastor's continuing concern for what is going on in the local church. Furthermore there is here an indication that the ex-pastors have suffered a great deal from the conflicting expectations of the laity.

> Laymen as a group still have a mass of stereotypes which they ought to get rid of. I mean stereotypes about the church and ministers. Politics and business are too holy for the church to handle—thus ensuring the irrelevance of the church. Ministers are a third sex, without any knowledge of or right to speak about psychology, sociology, government, business, industry, foreign affairs, or anything else in the real world. Most laymen, though, assume that their ignorance and prejudice give them a perfect right to thoughtlessly override the minister in the field of his expertise, the content and implications of the Christian faith.
>
> • • •
>
> Your minister does not have all the answers. He needs your help as much as you need his. He makes mistakes too. He wants most of all to help you. He needs your sympathetic understanding when he fails at times to measure up to what you expect of him. He appreciates very much your expression of gratitude when you know he has helped you.
>
> • • •
>
> Give the minister a right to his own views and don't use dependence of the minister on the congregation as pressure to keep the minister in line.

ATTITUDES

The ex-pastors give counsel relative to attitudes on the part of the laymen. *Be open* to the new world, new possibilities, new ways of doing things.

> *Don't be suspicious* of the new hymns, liturgy, sex attitudes, approaches to Christian education, cell organization of the church, etc. Don't cling so tightly to a building, when merger with a neighboring congregation would

benefit all and enable the church better to fulfill its mission in the community.

• • •

Don't be afraid to talk back. But if you have an open mouth, you also have a responsibility to have an open mind.

• • •

Speak out and ask the questions which are really troubling you.

• • •

Don't be satisfied with ushering and fund raising, but realize a compassion for the human race, following your pastor if he is interested in making a difference in this world.

• • •

Expect your minister to be an authentic person in the world. Help him to break out of his stained-glass cage.

• • •

Care! My wife was not in church for months and months but not one lay person who worked with me came to me and asked, ". . . , why doesn't . . . come to church?" Now in God's name, why? Not one.

Since the pastors in some deep sense have really rejoined the laity, it is not surprising to find among them a strong image of the laity.

You are the real ministers. Laymen should realize in greater numbers and greater depth that they are the church, and that its mission is theirs. Laymen get the idea that they hire the minister to be Christian for them. However dedicated, however energetic the minister, he simply cannot carry on all the human contact which the church ought to be making, and he continues his counseling (emergency) and preaching ministries as well. What I am saying is that laymen should recognize that the church's ministry is their responsibility, and should (with the minister's guidance and support) carry it out.

You must come to seriously realize and believe that you are the real ministers. The church is only an alive and relevant factor when you make it so—not in terms of weekly, institutional gatherings, but in terms of decisions and life. You must be willing to open up and let the church explore. You must urge the ministers to take the challenge of the world seriously. You must be honest in your questions and concerns, and aim at permitting the institutional church to be a place where you discover your real questions and concerns and examine them.

Turn on to the world. Although many of the ex-pastors strongly urge the laymen to carry a much larger share of the load in institutional maintenance of the church, the strongest emphasis is that the layman live out his commitment in his everyday life. The ex-pastors' perspective and their feelings are summarized by the admonition, "Turn on to the world, your ministry is there!"

A new understanding. Some of the men are able to surmount their anger at the system and their feelings of pain to take a fresh look at the layman. There is good feeling in this passage:

> Laymen are in need of as much understanding about the changing society as they can possibly absorb. I am more in sympathy with the layman today, I suspect, than before. He is facing a world in which the old values have changed, and he's not sure his former attitude of protest is going to do much good anymore. Now he doesn't know, he tends to make fewer judgmental comments in my conversation with him, and to do more searching for answers. The answers he is searching for, I feel, are less in what we say than in what we do.

The church and business are not the same. Few pastors and businessmen come to a meeting of the mind relative to the business of the church. Echoes of this real struggle are seen in this passage:

> The local church can profit immeasurably from your secular experience in business, industry, the arts, and sciences. The wisdom you have gained from your work outside the church is invaluable; however, do not construe the church as a branch office of your business. In some respects we can operate the church in a businesslike way, but in other respects the Christian church is different and you should be acutely aware of that which makes for its greatness. Respect that quality.
>
> • • •
>
> *Don't become a clergyman if you can possibly avoid it.* No one really understands what the role should be, ought to be, or could be. Expectations are impossible to fulfill.

Pastors' Counsel to Laymen

There is practically no difference in the counsel given by the ex-pastors to laymen and the counsel given by our control group of pastors. Both the feelings and perspective are very similar. There is a marked difference, however, in that the pastors frequently urge laymen to support the pastor and respect his office.

UNDERSTANDING THE ROLE OF THE PASTOR

> Don't expect divine perfection of a man who is forced to perform as a jack-of-all-trades and consequently is a master of none. No one can have expertise in all departments of the pastoral ministry.
>
> • • •
>
> Laymen need to understand the changing role of the pastor in today's culture. They also need to set realistic expectations for the man or woman they call their minister.
>
> • • •

Give your minister the privilege of being a man!—or woman!

* * *

Give a little consideration to understanding your pastor's unique problems in his ministry.

ATTITUDES

The same feeling of frustration is felt among the pastors as is evident among ex-pastors. The feelings behind these passages are every bit as strong as the words.

> Either put up, or shut up! Either take your commitment seriously or get out of the way.
>
> * * *
>
> Wake up and get moving! Stop expecting the minister to do everything you should rightfully do as fellow members of the church. There is so much to be done and so few of you who really care about anyone or anything other than yourself or what you own!
>
> * * *
>
> For Christ's sake, get with it!
>
> * * *
>
> Wake up! Say what you think. Don't wait until after the meeting. Be yourself. Be open. I'd rather have you cuss me out and be honest than smile sweetly while you murder me in your mind.
>
> * * *
>
> Your God is dead!

Help shape the future. Many of the pastors are really hooked on the belief that the local church has a strong responsibility in helping to shape the new world. They call the laity to share their vision. "Don't let the clergy and the old-style church leaders pull the wool over your eyes. Be creative. Dream great dreams for the church!"

Advice to Fellow Pastors from the Ex-Pastors

As data presented in this book will show the support system represented by fellow pastors did not hold up well for these ex-pastors. So it is understandable that there is considerable feeling relating to their brothers in the ministry. Some of the ex-pastors' advice to them is short:

> Stop bitching.
>
> * * *
>
> The cross is for real man.
>
> * * *
>
> Shut up and listen!
>
> * * *
>
> Relax, stop trying to impress your peers.

* * *

Stop climbing the bishop's ladder.

* * *

Stop giving pat answers.

* * *

Come on over. Have a scotch and tell me your troubles.

* * *

Quit being a stuffed shirt and act as a human being.

* * *

Get the hell out of your bag if you are turned off to the institutional church.

* * *

Get with it!

* * *

Think seriously of getting out!

* * *

Learn to do something else for a living or else do your present job better.

* * *

Stop selling out!

In the above counsel there is brotherly anger mixed with scorn. But there is a deeper dimension mixed with pain. Here the plea is made that pastors "encounter their neighbor minister more honestly. Express greater caring for him and stand up together with him." More than any other, this advice was given. And in the following counsel there is a strong note of caring.

Meet more frequently with other pastors. Discuss your problems frankly and openly with one another. Pray together. Give to one another the helpful understanding and support which can best come from others who are facing the same difficulties, problems, and frustrations. Plan together and talk over constructive programs, and share with each other helpful suggestions and activities which you have found to be of benefit.

* * *

One thing that I believe I caught a glimpse of is that there is a glimmer of need for mutual support in all of us, more need for this in some of us. Why hide it? It is not failure as a person to admit need to one another. Indeed, it could be Christian humility to realize this interdependence.

* * *

Ministers rarely give warm and strong support to each other in times of stress—most of them seem to ignore the crises which affect a neighboring pastor. Ministers become islands of parochial security or islands of devastation. They behave much like their churches: courteous regard but little support for any agony beyond the home and the parish boundaries.

* * *

The ministry is the loneliest job in the world, and with rare exception I found fellow pastors too absorbed in their own affairs to be concerned with their fellows. Pastors need to assume the role of something akin to father-confessors to one another. So much could be done in this respect to give comfort, aid, and understanding to a fellow pastor. This is an area where much could be done and isn't being done. The denominations should have a pastor unrelated to promotional schemes, etc. who would be available as a spiritual troubleshooter. He would be, not an answer man, but one who could come in and hear out the local pastor, absorb his problems, and offer a sympathetic and understanding ear.

• • •

Exert a little more compassion and understanding and concern to a brother who has made a mistake, corrected it, and proved himself after four and a half years of faithful ministry. If the clergy of the church cannot extend a forgiving hand, how can we expect laymen to?

Some General Counsel

Talk with the man dropping out. Listen to him.

I had excellent relationship with my fellow pastors until I accepted the present position. I still have with some. But some have been cold who had been my best friends before; they have tended to become punctilious about certain aspects of the pastoral relationship. Not one has ever visited with me about my reasons for taking the present action, least of all the church and ministry committee of our association, even after I suggested several times I was willing to do so.

• • •

One's fellow pastors who have fallen in the ecclesiastical battle should be befriended rather than shunned. Only a couple of ministers extended sympathy or even mentioned my plight. Oddly enough these were conservative ministers who had less in common with me than the mainstream of ministers.

• • •

Fellow pastors tend to be quite defensive in their relationship with those who are entering into new forms of ministry. Not only do we have little to talk about, but one gets the feeling that one has "lost status" by leaving the traditional ministry. The church talks with earnestness about its ministry to the world in the world, but when a minister actually goes into the world to minister in a nontraditional form, he speedily discovers that the structure of ecclesiastical fellowship and work simply has no place for him.

• • •

Cooperate with those in secular style ministries. *Seek out and become personally acquainted* with the other professional people in your community area who function in healing or protective capacities (e.g., social workers, public health nurses, probation officers, school counselors). They will broaden your understanding of the problems your people face and show you resources to which you can make meaningful referrals.

In the social service functions of your church don't let this become a do-it-yourself program. Prepare your church members to get involved themselves. Stay with them when they hit the gut-level problems of involvement.

• • •

You better read the newspaper alongside of the Bible every day if you expect to be able to speak a word that is important enough to be heard. Denominationalism is dead. The secular man will not listen for more than five minutes to anyone who seems to be promoting it. The ecumenical approach to worship and to social problems is the only course worth taking. Cooperation between churches and social service agencies needs to be developed so that the church will become a referral source and a helping resource to those agencies.

• • •

Lay aside protected economic status. Get out of the parsonage; buy your own house.

Seek more in-service training.

Get new skills in community organization, administration, counseling.

• • •

I would urge my fellow pastors to continue their studies and to *demand* regular opportunity to resist nitty-gritty cake-carrying in order to be able to study. Until I entered collegiate teaching, I had little opportunity to read. Too many people look to the clergy to be personnel managers, financiers, ad hoc business managers, errand boys, counselors, general do-gooders and angels—ad nauseam. Can one man do all this? I say that his first loyalty is to the development of his (and their) faith and his mind.

Many urge continuing to minister but making a living elsewhere.

PERSONNEL POLICIES—SALARY

After better than 25 years in the ministry, my decision is that all clergymen must be a Paul, a preacher, and a tentmaker. I have served for 25 years and have been able to accumulate $2,500 for retirement. I have worked, my wife has worked and is working now, and that is a small showing for 25 years of work. I cannot in good conscience advise a young person to enter the ministry. I have never received more than a common laborer's wage.

I earned more in 1948 operating a punch press than serving two churches. A carpenter in the present congregation earns better than $10,000, the wife stated. I do not know.

When a clergyman is young the congregation does not want you because you have no experience. When you are older the congregation does not want to listen to your experience and thinks you are too old.

A sister of mine is a teacher and stated, "The only way they can say thanks is by paying more; this is the only language they know." This is true of the clergy. When I first told my father I planned to go into the clergy, he said, "What do you want to be, a beggar?" I have learned that this is very true.

• • •

Learn some skill or profession by which you can make an honest living, then use your theological training and Christian commitment to be a man in the world where things are happening. Stop playing religious games. Overcome the delusion that the church offers contacts to you whereby you can "reach greater numbers for Christ" than you could in a secular setting. Recognize that this is a secular world—albeit influenced by the Spirit of Christ (almost wholly in unlikely, "secular" ways)—and join the human race.

• • •

Take a secular job and stay in their ministry only as a trained cadre to equip their fellow laymen to be secular saints. This was not possible for me in my last conventional parish and is rarely possible in the church as now constituted and understood by the laity.

Take sensitivity training so they can feel another's suffering. I was helped over a rough spot by a group of young ministers at a retreat house who met once a month and talked at gut level. They accepted me in love the first time I went and I was able to spill it all out. That was a religious experience!

• • •

You need better training especially in the area of leadership. You come out of the seminary prepared to fall into the rut existing in the churches and perpetuate existing institutional conformity.

• • •

Pastors should be trained in group dynamics. They also require discipline in personal devotional life to increase their religious insight and thereby to be capable of providing the example required among the laity.

• • •

You need much more understanding of interpersonal dynamics between people.

ADVICE TO THOSE THINKING ABOUT CHANGING

This counsel was not asked for but it appears through the papers sent in.

Stay with it as long as you can.
Slowly, carefully, weigh the alternatives of where and how you can best fulfill your ministry.
Take advantage of every opportunity for continuing education. If possi-

ble, work for a master's degree. Be aware that it takes a long time to make a change.

. . .

To those who have been able to maintain their vision in the midst of constant frustration: 1. Let us close ranks and support one another in the face of lay and executive attacks. 2. If the first recommendation is not acceptable—drop out with me and let them look for ministers till doomsday.

. . .

If you are in the ministry because it is a comfortable, secure occupation —get out.

. . .

If you are in the ministry because of a commitment to God, humanity, or because you have something to say and can say it well (and better yet, live what you are saying) stay with it, and more power to you.

. . .

Get out of the pastoral ministry.

. . .

The church is a great thing not to be in! The possibilities for fulfilling many of the goals shaped prior to seminary and formulated in seminary can often be fulfilled more effectively outside the church. What is most disturbing of all, the ministry has allowed itself to lose its own self-respect from the point of view of financial remuneration for actual hours and the amount of training needed; and, most important, in a vocation which should experience the maximum in creativity, there is probably the least possible within the normal structure of the church.

On reflection—to fellow pastors considering the "drop out" experience, I say: "Don't make the move until you have secured your vocational connection in advance. Once you move outside the cloister, neither the denomination nor the society accepts you; you are man without a country or credentials, and it means trying to carve out a place for yourself as if your training and experience mean nothing. Protect yourself, at this point, at all cost!"

Pastors' Counsel to Fellow Pastors

Again the counsel given by the control group of pastors is not much different from the counsel given by the ex-pastors. Their advice to their fellow pastors is also often on the same feeling level as that given by the ex-pastors.

Quit making the ministry a political jungle.

. . .

Be human.

. . .

Quit griping; become more positive.

• • •

Be open and frank with fellow pastors.

• • •

Take off your mask.

• • •

Get with it.

Jealousy appears to be a new factor. It was not mentioned at all by the ex-pastors but is frequently mentioned by the pastors.

The expression of need for fellowship and for caring often appears among the pastors, just as it did among the ex-pastors. "Let's support each other more." "Get to know me." There is also the emergence of the note that ministers need to organize professionally. "We should organize like the other professions—share and help one another." More pastors than ex-pastors are urging some form of union. One man already has the motto: "Never run when the hounds start up. Organize!"

One man ruminates in behalf of many: "My advice to myself too. Take time to nurture friendships among fellow pastors. I am lonely. But I, too, am 'so busy' I don't cultivate them either."

• • •

> *Don't cop out and yet stay in the ministry*. There are too many men who have sold out their personal integrity and have settled for giving their congregations the unchallenging ministry they seem to want. It is the old school of "Herr Pastor" which is holding the church back more than the laity.

Counsel of Ex-Pastors to Seminaries

There is almost total unanimity among the ex-pastors that their seminaries did not train them properly for the parish ministry. The complaints fall clearly into these categories: 1. Seminaries and local churches are out of phase. Many seminary professors are simply unaware of what goes on in a local church and the pressures under which the pastor exists. 2. The seminaries trained men cerebrally but did not give sufficient help in self-encounter, and did not give the necessary practical skills needed in this time.

OUT OF PHASE

Here is testimony from one of the men who was "trained at a seminary that had vision and courage to experiment with new and challenging forms of Christian ministry training which would address itself to the issues *now*." This is what he says:

> Were you aware of the fact that though we are trained for the twentieth century (and possibly the twenty-first) that our local parishes are not? Were you aware of the fact that though we were sensitized to the urgencies

of contemporary history, our parishes are not so sensitized? They can still focus their concerns on whether their minister spends his time holding the hands of, and serving tea to, old maids and wealthy widows. Are you aware of the fact that young men, thus trained, die just a little each day in the midst of this? You trained us to serve and minister to the living, and to celebrate the joy of living, but were you aware of the fact that we go out and find ourselves having to spend the great bulk of our time serving the dead? Were you also aware of the fact that if we do stand for something or minister to the living, that we will probably not have a parish for very long? (And after we are asked to leave, what do we do then? We were not trained for much else.)

My recommendations are that you change your curriculum to include a course on how to prostitute oneself gracefully, to sell one's soul with dignity, and to desensitize oneself with honor.

Still others speak of an anti-parish bias.

You Took Me on a Head Trip

Most of the men bear strong testimony to the fact that during seminary their training was cerebral. Many of them express keen appreciation for the courses which they experienced and for the dedication of the professors, but there is an overwhelming complaint that they were not taught the necessary practical skills.

This will come as no news to seminary professors or to pastors or to ex-pastors. A very strange phenomenon exists at most seminaries. Courses in the practical phases of the parish ministry are sometimes laughed at and have very low prestige value. Many of these are the very courses which are of greatest importance once one becomes a pastor of a church and faces the stark realities of heading a parish. A large number of seminaries have taken cognizance of this phenomenon and are seeking to fill the gap. The ex-pastors join many others who believe that the world has changed radically. They know that the institution must be updated, that leaders of an institution today must have specialized skills. They say simply, they didn't get them.

> I was entirely satisfied with my seminary and the work I did there, with the exception of one area of life and curriculum, and that was "field work." I recognize the value of "practical training" to supplement theoretical learning. Unfortunately nobody *trained* me to do anything. Whatever I learned, I learned by trial and error. More significantly, I was so stimulated by the teachers and students of the seminary, that I was reluctant to give up time to do this "practical work," presumed to be so necessary. I felt I would be doing enough of that in years to come anyway.

> • • •

> There was no training with respect to the hard realities of life when I went to school, no preparation concerning the seminarian's finances. There probably is now. I was in seminary between the old and the new order.

More of an effort should have been made to assess just where I belonged in the ministry. As far as practical aspects are concerned, I didn't even know how to conduct a funeral or baptize, or even begin to think of financial situations. I was top student in my class and green, green, green!

SOME COUNSEL THEY GIVE

Make pastoral preparation a threefold thrust: 1. Emphasize current geographic, social, and economic trends. 2. Place emphasis on community and congregational behaviorisms as these are related to the above indicated trends. 3. Continue striving to lay theological foundations, but especially seek to relate and bring these to bear upon 1 and 2 above.

It seems to me the so-called "revolution" in the church is occurring simply because some men have found an effective way of communicating the faith in related theological interpretations. However, where opposition and dissent is occurring, this is usually the result of men who are (a) ill trained in their own theological foundations, or, (b) not sufficiently trained in the art of communicating a particular theological thrust in terms of the environment of their pastorate. In a sense, it is a question of men being prepared in relation to the areas and environments where they shall be serving. I believe this to be less a problem of personal inclination or desire but more a delinquent initial training in the art of relative theological conversation and instruction.

• • •

Make clinical training in a hospital, prison, or juvenile home setting a seminary requirement (minimum three-month period). Basic elements of this experience would be exposure to people in crisis situations, contact with other professional disciplines concerned with healing or care, and the task of relating the implications of this experience to the students' own understanding of theology.

• • •

Tell the boys "the way it is" in churches. Teach how to understand the racist mind and war-mindedness. Teach a theology of social involvement. Root the student in contemplative practice in strength so he can stand a required intern year. Also, we need a lived-with rather than a taught-to faculty.

• • •

I would urge that the gulf which still exists between social work and the profession of the ministry be bridged by much more of the seminary curriculum being devoted to behavioral and social sciences including group dynamics, social action, and community organization and development. Social casework techniques could render pastoral calling much more efficient as part of the helping professions, and group work and community organization are tools which would render the church socially more relevant to the needs of our changing culture.

Cultivate and broaden fieldwork (secular world-oriented) and clinical-year program. Integrate church (seminary training) and world emphasis on theological training through some scheme such as six months in seminary and six months in secular and parish work, ministering in a scientific technological age.

• • •

Do not pass on to a congregation (by the granting of a degree) a student burdened with a severe personality disturbance. Require and give assistance.

Many of the ex-pastors gave this kind of counsel:

Involve all first-year students in group therapy to help them examine their motivation for entering the ministry, their feelings about it, etc. Then offer individual therapy to those wanting it—and those felt to need it too —during the second and third years while they are still in the "protected" atmosphere of the seminary where self-confrontation is not so threatening as in a parish. In this way you would help develop much more mature ministers, men and women able to work on a team ministry without being threatened by those with greater talents in one way or another.

Several of the ex-pastors urged *more careful selection of candidates and the utilization of testing procedures.*

Selection of candidates should be much more careful. In-depth questioning of candidates for psychological and emotional stability and maturity is vitally necessary.

• • •

Integrate the seminary community into the life of some great university. If the Christian is to go into the world *incognito,* the seminary cannot be aloof from the whole world of secular education. The seminary student must daily rub shoulders with and have to answer the embarrassing questions of the best students.

Some ex-pastors are very critical of the noninvolvement of seminary professors in the risk-taking business of involving the church in the world. Thus:

Dust out the cobwebs and come down off the hill. Get on the street where the action is! Put some flesh on the word that is so much bandied about in the safe classroom. How can the prophets be taught without your being prophetic?

• • •

Stop trying to train ministers. Train religious generalists to serve government, education, business, law, medicine. You are a gold mine being wasted.

Then there is the ex-pastor who has had it. His hope for the seminaries is gone. He simply says:

> The world needs new forms of ministry for which the current faculty cannot prepare others. *Close up,* and give the land to the poor! Infiltrate the colleges. Let ministers for churches be trained in a sort of apprenticeship.

Pastors' Counsel to the Seminaries

Just as with the ex-pastors, the most unanimous note struck by the pastors is that their seminary did not train them in the practical skills necessary to being a leader in today's church. Many say that they got a good theoretical training but that the skill training was utterly missing. When they talk about the practical skills they tend to be more specific than the ex-pastors and speak in terms of change-agentry, clinical training, conflict management, group therapy, leadership training, business administration.

There is also a strong feeling among the pastors that seminaries have an anti-parish bias and that most of the professors do not know what goes on in a local church. They are still working from old remembrances of another day; another model of the pastoral ministry was still possible. Many of them urge that professors in seminaries take sabbatical leaves in parishes and learn what is going on.

There is a strong plea from among the pastors that seminaries pay more attention to the behavioral sciences and the derivative skills.

1. Intensive training in handling conflict and use of creative conflict as agent of change.

2. More stress on urban ministry with necessary "tooling" to minister in this secular age.

3. Training in how to "theologize" using biblical and historical theology perspectives.

Except for the mention of devotional and spiritual guidance, the counsel of the pastors to the seminaries sounds much like the counsel given by the ex-pastors.

Advice to Church Administrators from the Ex-Pastors

Church administrators are the outward and visible sign of the church system. The ex-pastors feel that the system has failed them—failed to give them adequate support, failed to use their talents. They are essentially angry at the system. It follows that they are angry at the administrators too.

Many of the ex-pastors feel a lack of relationship to the administrators and see them as unnecessary baggage. Thus:

> I never had a conversation with any of these.

• • •

Very little vital relation with me in pastoral work. Mostly keep occupied with the machinery to keep it going.

· · ·

Get rid of most of them! However effectual they may be in some sense of the word, they are top-heavy financial liabilities and definite deterrents to the best interest of genuine ecumenicity.

· · ·

I never have had any but the most perfunctory relationship with conference or national staff. This used to make me furious. Now I couldn't care less.

· · ·

When you ask for help of persons at the national level you feel—whether it is true or not—they don't really give a damn. I tried for two years to find a place within the church in the field of education. I finally gave up and looked elsewhere. I was accepted by a secular-education research council with less formal credentials than my own church would accept.

A few of the men expressed strong appreciation for administrators.

These have been, by and large, helpful. I would say to continue what you are doing in the area of educating all of us about our world. As I moved to consider my present position in a community program for the aged, the conference staff gave much counsel and encouragement. They have generally indicated a better grasp of the world in which we live, and have maintained a good sustaining relationship with me when the local pastors at times became difficult.

But this kind of expression of appreciation was more the exception than the rule. Others with a different perspective said:

They are too busy and too harassed to be good listeners. National offices are impervious to suggestions, and not open to evaluation of ideas other than those which are within the present patterns. All the brave talk to the contrary, the current new thrusts are not new—but are the rehash of the last quarter century. This is a time for vision and courageous action which has seemed to be lacking during my span of years.

Many expressed the strong opinion that church administrators were not supportive when they got in trouble.

The national, state, and local denominational organizations are much too derelict in their obligations to back up and sustain the local pastor. In all my difficulties I felt I was completely alone so far as these were concerned.

In view of this perspective and these feelings, four of the men gave some very short counsel: "Resign." Still others said:

> They need to decide whether or not they wish to continue the present UCC attitude of throwing the minister to the wolves in case of problems on the assumption that there must be something wrong with him. In particular, conference executives have power of professional life or death over ministers, and in our system, as opposed to the episcopal polity, absolutely no responsibility for ministers, nor accountability to anyone in their exercise of this power. It seems to me that this guarantees 100 percent negative attitude on their part. Ministers come and go, but the lay people remain—so naturally, don't worry about the clergy.
>
> •　•　•
>
> Superintendents seem to be all ears to hear grievance about a pastor, rather than supporting him.
>
> •　•　•
>
> I am aware of the terrible load of administration upon them, but I would have given anything simply to have had any one of them as a friend I could turn to.

Church administrators should have more respect for the local church and its minister. Once again it seems surprising that this should be a primary concern of the ex-pastor. But more counsel of the ex-pastors to administrators centered around this than any other.

> As chairman of a conference committee on the ministry for four years, I was privileged to consult with numerous pastors who felt utterly isolated between 75 percent of their laity on the one hand and professional colleagues on the other—including conference and national staff. They felt neither was sufficiently sensitive to their needs.
>
> •　•　•
>
> They need not feel that they are of a higher order and thus feel superior to parish ministers. They like to live high, hobnobbing with fellow executives, attending big meetings all the time because that is where the important people are, thus not having time or any interest in being a minister to ministers or in giving counsel on church programs or to individual ministers as persons.

Some expressed no trust.

> Stop demeaning the role of preaching and the suburban pastor. Emphasize continuing education. Get in touch with the local church. Cease your politics and power plays within your organization. Pastors no longer trust your ministry.

Some of the counsel was short.

Drop dead.

. . .

There just aren't enough of these positions for all of us who want out of the parish ministry.

. . .

You are about as remote as you can possibly get!

. . .

You are useless.

. . .

Stop the bullshit.

. . .

You are corrupt.

. . .

Stop kidding yourselves.

. . .

Eliminate stuffing of the shirt.

. . .

Resign your office. Go back to the pastorate.

. . .

Quit putting out so many programs.

GENERAL SUGGESTIONS

That they not compromise the truth in order to save the existing structure; that they not sacrifice a minister in order to placate a congregation; that they be less defensive, more democratic, and less prejudicial in a crisis.

. . .

A period of change is a tough time for an administrator. During such a time we urgently need leaders, and the two are not always the same. Leadership is that element which can carry new thoughts and courageous designs into the world of reality. Leadership has the courage and the wisdom to say No to sentimentality and self-worship, and Yes to vision and self-sacrifice. At this point we could do with less administration and more leadership.

. . .

As a sociologist, I would urge the members of the upper structure of the church to recognize the fantastic changes that are taking place in the American social structure, and to gear their efforts to that change. We all must realize that unless the Christian church modernizes and updates itself, it will become an anachronism. I don't think that the publishing of slick denominational journals alone will accomplish this end. A good deal of bushbeating will be needed.

. . .

Emphasize new forms of ministry. The world needs new forms of ministry, not institutionalists and incognito. To develop them would be a better stewardship than keeping the old alive.

• • •

I just got worn out trying to get situated in another parish, though the time was ripe for me to leave.

• • •

Develop a better placement system.

• • •

Make a special effort to help clergy return to the parish ministry.

Establish a clergy employment agency.

The fact that hundreds and thousands of priests, pastors, and nuns are leaving the cloisters indicates many things. One prime factor is their need for assistance to retain their own integrity in the finding of a place of vocation in the community outside the institution. At present there is no vehicle to accomplish this. Each is thrown on his own to start from the bottom again. Establish a clergy employment agency!

• • •

Challenge people for more money. You're too . . . timid.

• • •

Be more ecumenical.

• • •

Develop more programs to attract the young.

• • •

Be open to the nonconformist. Give the nonconformist a chance. He may not fit into the finely balanced structuring of your setup or program, but he may be tuned in to a drumbeat you need to hear.

• • •

Quit being so damned embarrassed and defensive about pastors who leave the parish ministry. Instead of seeing this as loss, or giving these displaced ministers the silent treatment, try to see this new development as opportunity. These men who have had the courage to make the change may be your most imaginative and creative persons. Dare to hear what they are saying! Rejoice that now theologically trained men are dispersed through the secular world in key positions. What an opportunity! But don't try to "win" them back to traditional worship and forms. Help them instead find new forms of community life in which they can participate with joy and enthusiasm.

Wider vision needed.

The church administrators need the wider vision of where the organizational patterns of the denomination are leading in terms of the function of the local church and the church's many other forms of ministry. *The inability to provide the ideological framework for the conduct of the church is perhaps the largest failing* that I see in church administrators.

Set new priorities.

We must be fearless about setting new priorities in the expenditure of funds. Far too much goes into mission aid for the creating and maintaining of pastoral service stations. Much of our process in starting new churches is a tragic extending of the good old American way of life, a reinforcement of the style which makes suburbia a haven for self-interest —a place of refuge from war and the injustices of our cities. These starts have made it difficult for concerned Christians to rock the institution's boat. We also have much nostalgia about the need for older mission-aided projects. We pump great volumes of money into pipelines to keep "ministries" going in various towns and central cities. But these hand-holding operations deceive those served and do nothing to effect social change.

One of the ex-pastors reaches for his Bible and allows it to shape his advice to church administrators. "Awake! Be on the alert! Your enemy the devil, like a roaring lion, prowls around looking for someone to devour." (See 1 Peter 5:8–9.)

Pastors' Counsel to Church Administrators

It is understandable why ex-pastors are angry at church administrators. At least it can be rationalized by administrators. But when we note that the control group of pastors is even more angry, church administrators had best sit up and take notice.

Except on the anger level there is practically no difference between the counsel of the ex-pastors and the pastors which is given to administrators.

Some warm statements appear in the reporting. "I think our denominational leaders are giving us excellent direction." But such statements are rare. Rather, the reporters strike the same note as the ex-pastors.

Lack of relationship.

Too many chiefs and not enough Indians best fits any suggestions in this area. Administrators in general are too far removed and too little known by the people.

• • •

Who are they?

Lack of support.

Church administrators urge local pastors out on a limb. When trouble ensues, they tend to react, "Well, he must have done something wrong."

• • •

Not sufficient rapport with the local churches and the grass roots. Most denominational programs come one way, from the top down.

• • •

Conference ministers should back up local ministers more than they do. They tend to take the side of the local congregation and to protect them whenever there are vital issues at stake.

• • •

When the church I was serving refused to declare church membership open to all (race issue), I resigned. From the president of the church I received a note of condolence saying that the denomination could give me a few bucks to tide me over until I found work. From the placement office of the denomination I got a letter telling me I shouldn't have resigned until I got a new job because it was very hard to find pulpits for radicals who resigned rashly. From my conference executive I received a visit to tell me that he would prefer for me to move out of this conference rather than rock the boat. If it had not been for laymen who roused up, shook that church good, and caused a real change in direction, I would have left the pastorate and it would have been because this damned bureaucracy we've developed is so bold on paper, and so hamstrung and unconcerned in action. Since then my view has been that the job is mine and I'd better do it my way on my resources rather than rely on the "brass." I also found that you play this game one of two ways—either by politics and a climb to the ranks of the officers—or as the spirit guides knowing you'll stay at the bottom.

Church administrators should have more respect for the local church and its minister. Just as in the case of the ex-pastors, this counsel appeared most often.

Counsel in short form. Counsel in short form appeared often in the pastors' reporting.

Stop speaking out of both sides of your mouth. You urge prophetic, creative ministry, yet judge us by old statistical values. You have us in a trap.

• • •

Quit justifying your existence by sending out such questionnaires as this. Admit you are parasites rather than necessities in the church; also admit that the pastors are on the firing line and are bearing the brunt of the load, and that the top brass only increases the load on the pastoral ministry.

• • •

Learn to listen!

• • •

Lead, pioneer, but don't get so far out in front that the people can't see where you are going.

* * *

Stop making me a current expense while calling fat-assed desk people who play golf on Sunday morning, mission people.

General suggestions—church administrators should take sabbaticals in the parish. This counsel appeared often and involved a variety of suggestions—1 in every 3 years, 1 in every 5, 3 in 10, and so forth.

Quit worrying so much about support, quit pushing programs (instead teach skills), spend more time calling on fellows not in crisis; spend enough time together with the staff so that personal problems among members can be dealt with effectively. Evaluate programs with real instead of assumed data.

* * *

Drastically cut printing and postage expenses. The huge volume which comes to my desk is far too great for a busy pastor to deal with conscientiously.

* * *

More careful selection for ordination and more supportive relationship to pastors who are in the tough and less desirable situations. Many of these situations have the power to ruin a good pastor.

* * *

Pay more attention to the small church.

2 / THE RESEARCH

Trusting that the reader has been thoroughly hooked by his sudden immersion into the counsel of pastors and ex-pastors, we offer a brief but necessary interlude before moving into a summary of principal findings (chapter 3). This research grew out of the need to know. To learn *from* ex-pastors was not sufficient, we also had to learn about them. Under the leadership of Howard E. Spragg and Gerald J. Jud, conferences in New York, Cleveland, Chicago, and San Francisco were scheduled for weekends in May and June 1968. The conferences themselves provided the occasion for gathering much of the data, and they shaped the interpretation of the data by their impact on the researchers' thoughts and feelings.

As an interlude telling how the study was done, chapter 2 is divided into five sections:

1. The design and pretesting of instruments
2. The gathering of the study sample
3. The collection of data
4. The experiences of the conferences and interviews
5. The delicate problem of nomenclature

1. The Design and Pretesting of Instruments

The original "Think Tank" (described in the Preface) gave rise to a smaller design committee made up of Gerald Jud, Genevieve Burch, Earl Brewer, and Edgar Mills. The group searched the literature of their respective fields, gathering and refining both ideas and research instruments relating to career change, organizational analysis, and the professional ministry. It was clear from the beginning that there would be two primary sources of the study design: (a) career development theory and (b) the sociology of occupations. The references mentioned in chapters 4 and 5 reflect our indebtedness to many workers in these fields. However, nearly everything previously done was tangential to the central theme of the study: why ministers change careers.

We early decided to use three types of data: (a) paper and pencil questionnaires, (b) private interviews, and (c) the conference sessions themselves. In order to provide advance data for the planning of the conferences, the questionnaire portion was divided into two parts, the first of which would be mailed to former pastors with the letter of invitation. The other part of the questionnaire and the private interview would be completed during the conferences. The questionnaires and interview guides as used are in Appendix A.

Part I of the advance questionnaire asked for the counsel of respondents to various groups in the life of the church. As soon as the returned questionnaire arrived at the National Council of Churches' Department of Research it was given a code number and the first part torn off and sent to Dr. Jud at the United Church of Christ headquarters. That data constitutes the basis for chapter 1 of this volume.

The purpose of the remainder of the first questionnaire was to gather basic personal information about the ex-pastor, to provide "timeline" knowledge of his career, and to answer pressing questions about the ex-pastor's current self-understanding, his theological point of view, and his reference and support systems. Because the seminal think tank was held at the end of December and the conference invitations had to go out at the beginning of March, the first questionnaire which was to accompany the invitations was never adequately pretested. It contained little, however, that had not successfully been used in earlier studies.

The second questionnaire was of a slightly different character, designed particularly to get evaluative data on the ex-pastor's last church position, the types of work which he enjoyed and close friendships he made, and his judgments about the reasons for his leaving. We also attempted to confirm types of theological change. This questionnaire was pretested by mailing it to a small selected sample of men from other denominations who had formerly been pastors.

The interview was to be of about one-hour duration and to deal with four topics: (a) the present situation and what changes have occurred in the ex-pastor's life since leaving church employment, (b) the process of deliberating, searching, and deciding on the move, (c) the experiences which led up to the move during his last church position, and (d) his feelings about his future. Mrs. Burch pretested the interview guide by using items from it in her master's dissertation study during the winter and spring of 1968.

The design committee laid preliminary plans for a comparison sample of UCC ministers currently in church employment to receive a comparable questionnaire at a later time. In the fall of 1968, with the cooperation of Dr. Harold Wilke and the Council for Church and Ministry, a 5 percent systematic random sample was taken of all UCC clergy in active ministry, and a questionnaire was prepared, consisting of the material in the two questionnaires completed by ex-pastors. This instrument is also included in Appendix A.

2. The Gathering of the Study Sample

The names of the UCC men who have withdrawn from the pastoral ministry were gathered from the conference executives, since it is their responsibility each year to report to the national office the names of ministers with standing. More than any others, they would know the names of those who had changed careers. We found them exceedingly cooperative and very interested in the project. Of the 383 names submitted, 13 were excluded as not fitting the sample definition. Thus our list consisted of 370 ex-pastors, which we estimate includes at least 80 percent of the total population of such persons. A copy of the letter sent to conference executives is in Appendix A, as is also a copy of the letter inviting ex-pastors to attend one of the four weekend conferences.

3. The Collection of Data

Of the 370 ex-pastors invited, 241 (65.1%) returned the first questionnaire which had accompanied the letter. A total of 231 usable replies were processed and are used in this report. Replies were sent to the National Council of Churches' Department of Research where they were partially coded and the data made available to the conference team for their guidance. Subsequent data coding and processing were handled at the Washington office of the Ministry Studies Board for all of the instruments.

Two hundred four ex-pastors actually registered for one of the regional conferences, and 149 attended. The necessity to arrange interviews of one hour or more with all participants during a brief weekend without keeping them from the sessions was a difficult problem. The researchers felt strongly that skilled and experienced interviewers should do all the interviews, and that there should be quiet and comfortable facilities with no time pressure during the contact period. On the other hand, the problem of employing that many interviewers and transporting them across the country for four conferences created an impossible budget strain. Moreover, there was much benefit to be gained by bringing seminary professors, denominational officials, and others into the interview situations to encounter in depth the experiences of ex-pastors. As usually happens in such situations, a compromise was agreed upon, in which interviewers would consist of volunteer professionals drawn from the areas in which the conferences were held, and trained by the researchers. Because so much negative feeling was attached to conference ministers and other local denominational leadership, they were excluded from interviewing, but national staff were expected to participate whenever possible. A two-hour training period was scheduled in advance of each of the conferences, during which interviewers covered the material in detail, certain cautions were given, and sensitive points discussed.

With these preparations, the interviewing proceeded reasonably well, and the interviewers felt that the experience was highly beneficial to them. Of the 149 persons who attended the conferences, 3 refused to be interviewed at all, 3 could not be scheduled for a variety of reasons, 4 were women,* and 8 interviews were done

---

* Because the careers of women are so different from those of men, and because there were too few women to make them a subgroup in the analysis, we chose instead to discuss them separately. This is done in chapter 3, pp. 56–58.

in a manner that makes the data unusable for our purposes. The resulting sample of 131 interviewed men constitutes the core of the data for this volume.

The 5 percent comparison sample mentioned earlier consisted of 452 active UCC clergy, of which 290 (64.2%) returned questionnaires. Of these, 20 proved to be in secular employment, 8 were retired, 3 were women, and 9 were undeliverable or otherwise ineligible according to the definition of the sample, leaving a total of 250 usable comparison pastors.

The possibility existed that our results would be biased because our data represented only part of the UCC clergy in secular work. To check this, we selected at random approximately 17 percent of the ex-pastor nonrespondents, along with a similar proportion of men who registered for the conferences but did not either show up or cancel in advance. These 31 persons were to be interviewed. For a variety of reasons, data were actually collected on only 20. Three could not be located, making an appointment with 3 proved impossible, 4 refused to be interviewed, and 1 failed to complete the written instruments. These interviews were carried out in a manner similar to the earlier ones, except that respondents were interviewed in their homes or other nearby places. This was done during the fall and winter following the conferences.

Comparing these 20 nonrespondents and no-shows with ex-pastors, we found that in age, marital status, college, seminary and denominational background, and attitude toward being in the ministry, the groups were alike. The nonrespondent/no-show sample had entered the ministry 1.7 years younger, held one position more, served 2.8 years longer, and been out of church work one year longer, on the average, than the ex-pastors. They were making about $1,000 less per year when they left. The two groups had about the same number of advanced degrees, but nearly half the degrees of the nonrespondents/no-shows were in education. A correspondingly larger proportion are now in educational work; and none are in labor, military, or science occupations.

In general, the nonrespondent/no-show men were slightly more concerned with job problems—money, use of own strengths, availability of appropriate work— and less concerned with family problems. They resemble ex-pastors and pastors in reference and support orientations, but received even less support from fellow UCC clergy and denominational executives. The pull of secular job opportunities and the push of dissatisfaction with parish work were slightly stronger. Otherwise, task enjoyment, job satisfaction, and reasons for leaving are quite similar.

A postcard survey of the 162 nonresponding pastors brought 71 returns (43.8%). They proved to be similar to pastors in the proportion of whites to nonwhites, males to females, and parish to nonparish clergy. As a group, their median age was 54.7 years—over 11 years higher than that of the pastors. This suggests that our study sample of pastors may be younger than UCC ministers as a whole, reflecting fewer of the concerns of clergy above 50. Nonrespondents' reasons for not returning the study questionnaire include 19 who were hostile ("too time-consuming," "such studies are meaningless"), 16 who said they *had* returned the questionnaire (but whose responses were never received), 15 to whom the study did not apply (retired, out of the country, out of church employment),

10 who mislaid the instrument or did not remember receiving it, 6 who confessed to laziness or procrastination, and 5 who gave no reason.

This review of the response bias data suggests that our ex-pastors may be biased somewhat toward those who left because of family problems and may include fewer than expected who had primarily job and money reasons for leaving. They also may underrepresent educational work among former pastors, and they appear to understate the inadequacy of the peer support system. Our pastors' sample apparently overrepresent the younger UCC ministers, the effect of which may be to make them *more* like the ex-pastors, since the latter tend to be slightly younger. In any case, these sources of bias should be borne in mind as the data are presented, but they do not, in our opinion, invalidate any of the arguments or conclusions of the book.

The questionnaire data were processed and coded in the Ministry Studies Board office under the direction of Margaret Brown, Polly Hendrick, and Janet Morse. Genevieve Burch developed the codes for open-end interview questions, using a pattern code method which takes corroborative data from several items and develops a single measure from them. Digitek scanner sheets were used to prepare the data for computer processing, and standard frequency and cross-tabulation programs developed by Dr. Ramon Henkel at the University of Maryland were used.

4. The Experiences of the Conferences and Interviews

Each of the four regional conferences began on Friday afternoon and ended at noon Sunday. Ex-pastors were guests of the Board for Homeland Ministries, as were the leadership teams that conducted the interviews and joined in the conference sessions. The New York and Chicago conferences were held in seminary facilities, while in Cleveland a public hotel was used and in San Francisco an isolated church conference center. The largest group—53—gathered in New York; Chicago drew 46, and 25 each came to Cleveland and San Francisco.

The purpose of the conferences was to do *disciplined listening* in order to learn from ex-pastors and to gain important data about them. Because we did not wish to give the impression that we had called them together to "do them good" or to inveigle them back into the parish ministry, we stressed the fact that the conferences were not set up as therapeutic experiences. Rather we wanted to learn from the ex-pastors and to give each man an opportunity to express as clearly and in as much detail as possible the dynamics of his life and professional career. We would have an opportunity together to discuss issues which were of primary concern to them.

The group structure of the conferences was oriented around plenary sessions and small "issue" groups. In the first plenary (Friday evening), the group was asked to define the issues which were important to them. Out of these, the most important issues were to be drawn, and the remaining four small groups and plenary sessions were devoted to these.

During the Chicago conference, for example, the following issues were listed by participants as important *:

1. What are the assumptions behind all the questionnaires we are asked to fill out?

2. How do we see our roles as ministers in nonchurch institutions?

3. How can we deal with the "matching problem"—matching men with work?

4. The issues of clerical power.

5. The theology of the church.

6. The relation of denominational officials to local pastors.

7. Clues from the "world." "Can we bridge between the church and the world?"

8. Personal and family life.

9. The church as a middle-class establishment.

10. Should theological education be more professionally oriented? What is its relation to other disciplines? How does one develop the artistic skills of ministering as a professional?

11. The growing agnostic and humanistic basis of society. Does this convert the theological endeavor into a philosophic endeavor?

12. The possibility of economic independence for clergy.

13. Being "put out" of the church—talents not being used.

14. Ultimacy of human values (in distinction from theological values).

15. Models and styles of becoming "anonymous Christians."

16. Broadening theological education—the need for cross-disciplinary sensitivity.

17. "Who am I as a clergyman in a nonchurch job?"

18. How do we transcend the language pattern to deal with the issues?

19. Theological confusion. Or is there any validity to theology?

Although the conferences differed considerably in mood and makeup, this list of issues is typical of the concerns of all four.

Prior to their coming to the conferences many of the men had expressed their great appreciation that the institutional church had at last taken some recognition of them, and this note of appreciation remained steady throughout. However, the length of the conferences and the format did not take an important dimension sufficiently into account. Many ex-pastors have been seriously wounded by the system. They have suffered a great deal and they are justifiably angry about it. It is possible to be appreciative and angry at the same time. Representatives of "the establishment," who had been responsible for setting up the conferences, became convenient targets for the angry feelings about the system. The conferences, however, had not been set up primarily to get at feelings but rather to learn from the

* We are indebted to Dr. Sidney D. Skirvin of Union Theological Seminary (N.Y.) for his astute summary and analysis of the Chicago conference: "Analysis of the Third 'Withdrawal' Conference of the UCC" (mimeo).

men and to gather data. In all four of the conferences the groups often abandoned the agreed-upon issues in order to get at some deep expression of feeling. Since the conference leaders were not "uptight" about agenda, the occasion provided opportunity for the venting of feelings. Angry feelings and hurt feelings and distrustful feelings were much in abundance. In the Chicago conference the members of the team were asked at length to leave so that the ex-pastors could meet alone. The New York conference concluded with a vigorous argument about whether the researchers and the national staff should be allowed full power to decide how to use the data. It became clear in the course of the conferences that other occasions need to be provided in the future to fulfill on a feeling level what was attempted on a cerebral level.

In spite of the strong feelings involved, an awareness of common concern pervaded the conferences. This was evident in the response to interviews which had to be scheduled at mealtimes, late at night, and between meetings. Nearly all the participants were cooperative and even eager to tell their story. Many of them brought along papers which they had written about their experiences or views. A great deal of feeling was expressed during the interviews, and many of the interviews lasted beyond their allotted time. For some, these personal contacts probably were the most helpful part of the conferences.

5. The Delicate Problem of Nomenclature

What do we call them? One of the names suggested for this book was "Pastors Who Quit." Chills ran up our collective spines at this thought, recalling the urgency with which conference participants and others insisted that they have *not* left the ministry. A Cleveland man said, "I haven't quit, I'm carrying on a lover's quarrel with the church." In Chicago, another said, "We didn't leave the ministry. The ministry left us." Still others argued vigorously for a distinction between leaving the pastorate and rejecting the ministry. "Dropout" became a dirty word.

We are heartily in accord with this view as it applies to most of our respondents. Unfortunately, it raises awkward problems of terminology. What *do* we call them? Our first questionnaire, sent with the letter of invitation to the conferences, was delicately titled: A Questionnaire for the Clergy in Nonecclesial Employment. This timid prose could not continue, however, if only because we couldn't keep saying "nonecclesial clergy." "Dropout" kept creeping in—it rolls nicely off the tongue. We discussed it more often than we would have liked and finally decided that the term ex-pastors states most precisely and with least prejudice who our respondents are. The chief disadvantage of this term is that an important minority of respondents were in nonparish ministries or on parish staffs when they entered secular work, which suggests that ex-pastors may be too narrow a term. However, only three had never served in a local church, which may help to justify its use.

Whatever its defects, however, we have used the term ex-pastors because its affective neutrality may allow our findings to be heard without triggering the tender feelings of those on both sides of the arguments about ordination and the meaning of ministry. We have been through those arguments in each of the four conferences, and we have our own opinions, some of which will become clear in the chapters to follow. Our plea, however, is that the reader not get hung up on the *words* we have used (or not used) but that he open himself to the *findings* presented. They alone are the justification for this book.

When we speak of *ex-pastors,* therefore, we mean persons who formerly were employed as ordained ministers in religious organizations but who now earn their living outside religious institutions. We use the term pastors similarly to include not only parish ministers but all ordained men in our comparison sample who earn their livings within religious organizations. This latter term we take to include seminaries and the religion departments of colleges and universities.

Having thus tried to avoid the monsters and the whirlpools of our highly charged topic, we fervently hope that this study will make it easier for others to thread the passage in future research.

3 / SUMMARY OF FINDINGS

What are the ex-pastors like? We could answer this variable by variable. We could print table after table with numbers and percentages. After forcing the reader to wade through many such pages, we would then explain that on most variables there is little difference between ex-pastors and pastors.

Instead, we have omitted most of the tables from this general summary chapter and have reserved the most technical prose for chapters 4 and 5. Tables summarized but not reproduced here have been included in Appendix B for the more persevering. (When a table appearing in Appendix B is referred to in the text, its number is preceded by the letter B.) We have included a few tabular presentations where the data would have been difficult to summarize in words alone, or where the differences presented seem particularly important to explore in detail.

Comparison of ex-pastors with our sample of current pastors constitutes the first major part of this chapter. In the second part, we summarize the way ex-pastors describe their decision to leave church employment and the factors leading up to it. In the last section, the major conclusions of this and subsequent chapters are briefly presented.

Ex-Pastors and Pastors

Who are the ex-pastors, and how different are they from men currently in church ministries? The ex-pastors certainly don't consider themselves as having "left the ministry," a description which only 13.9 percent accept. Sixty-two percent of the ex-pastors see themselves as performing a ministry in their current jobs (Table B1). Pastors also seem open to such a broad understanding of ministry, since nearly half describe themselves as "permanently in the ministry but not committed to staying in the pastorate." About 1 in 20 is planning to enter specific nonparish or secular work. Less than 40 percent describe themselves as "permanently in the pastorate."

WHERE DO THEY COME FROM?

Pastors and ex-pastors alike reflect the increasingly urbanized character of America. Among both of our groups, about two fifths have grown up in metropolitan areas, another two fifths in places of less than 10,000 people, and the remaining one fifth in small cities of less than 50,000 (Table B2). In 1935 Douglass and Brunner reported that of 1,800 pastors, nearly two thirds were from towns and villages, a fourth from small cities, and only an eighth from metropolitan areas. Pastors and ex-pastors also appear to be similar in their socioeconomic background, with about 1 in 8 coming from a clergyman's family, and the remainder broadly distributed among fathers in many occupations. Slightly more ex-pastors are from white-collar families and slightly fewer from blue-collar families than the pastors, but the differences are not impressive (Table B3). Less than 3 percent of both are nonwhite (Table B4).

On two counts, however, the ex-pastors differ in interesting ways from the pastors. As Table 1 shows, more than half the ex-pastors transferred in from other denominations, showing considerably more interdenominational mobility than the pastors, of whom 61.6 percent have always been in the United Church of Christ or its constituent denominations. In all, ex-pastors report 203 denominational changes thus far in their careers, while pastors report only 108 such changes. (Details are in Table B5.)

Also, ministers beginning as Evangelical and Reformed members are less likely to move to secular employment. Only 1 in 7 ex-pastors began as E & R members but approximately one third of the present pastors began in the E & R denomination. Approximately one fourth of both groups began in the Congregational Christian branch of the UCC.

Another point of difference is in college majors (Table B6). More than a third of the ex-pastors majored in the sciences, either natural or social, whereas little more than one fifth of the pastors did. By contrast, religion and helping occupations (social work, education) tend to have interested pastors more than ex-pastors as college majors.

HOW DID THEY GET INTO THE MINISTRY?

The median * age of decision to enter the ministry was between 20 and 21 years of age for both groups (Table B7), and their age at ordination was 28 years for ex-pastors and 27.4 for pastors (Table B8). It may be of some importance that pastors are clustered in the 25–29 age bracket at ordination, while ex-pastors are more openly distributed from 20 to 34. About a fourth of each group (Table 41, p. 113) had worked full-time in other occupations before entering the ministry.

The seminary backgrounds of ex-pastors (Table B9) show that Eden graduates are considerably less likely to appear among the ex-pastors and Chicago grad-

---

* A median marks the "middle one" of a distribution. Half of the respondents fall below the median and half above. Medians are used in this report rather than means because they are less subject to distortion by extreme values of age, salary, etc.

uates are more likely. Otherwise, there were no important differences between particular seminaries attended by the two groups. There is a slight tendency for men who attended seminaries of other denominations to appear more often among the ex-pastors, reflecting their higher interdenominational mobility. Between 3 and 4 percent of both groups did not attend seminary at all. When asked what they were seeking when they went to seminary, ex-pastors were more likely to check "seeking a *faith*" or "already a believer and seeking a *vocation*" than pastors were (Table B29). On the other hand, pastors were more likely to be "already clear about vocation and seeking to *prepare* for it." The meaning of these figures is discussed in chapter 4.

Table 1. Denominational Change and Career Change

	EX–PASTORS		PASTORS	
	NUMBER	PERCENT	NUMBER	PERCENT
Always UCC, Congregational Christian, or Evangelical & Reformed	100	43.3	154	61.6
Transferred from other denominations	126	54.5	95	38
No response	5	2.2	1	0.4
	231	100.0	250	100.0

WHAT WERE THEIR MINISTRIES LIKE?

On the whole, the ministries of ex-pastors and pastors do not appear to have been very different. A general discussion of task enjoyment is in chapter 4. By way of summary here, ex-pastors and pastors agree that counseling and preaching are the most enjoyable parts of the ministry and that conducting meetings, planning programs, and working at denominational duties are the least highly enjoyed (Table 18, p. 73). They differ in two respects. First, pastors enjoy most of the role tasks more than ex-pastors, even though in most ways the order of preference is the same. The only significant exception to this is that ex-pastors enjoyed community activity considerably more than pastors. Second, there are tasks which pastors seemed to enjoy *much* more than ex-pastors did: helping individuals to commitment, preaching, and general calling. Perhaps such tasks are the nucleus of a core role which differentiates ex-pastors from pastors. More research is needed on that point.

Chapter 4 also discusses job satisfaction. We asked for satisfaction ratings on several aspects of the minister's life and work, ranging from his salary and family time to the more intrinsic rewards of the work (Table 2).

The most striking difference between the two groups is in the item which both agree was most satisfying: "freedom to preach and act as you see fit." Nearly three fourths of the pastors indicated high satisfaction with this, but less than half the ex-pastors did. Few in either group were highly satisfied with members' willingness to carry out their Christian witness in the world, or members' willingness

Table 2. High Satisfaction with Aspects of the Ministry *

How Well Satisfied Are You With:	EX–PASTORS (131)		PASTORS (250)	
	Number	Percent	Number	Percent
1. Members' willingness to study and be trained?	17	13.0	32	12.8
2. Your own freedom to preach and act as you see fit?	58	44.3	184	73.6
3. The amount of time you have for family and private life?	23	17.6	74	29.6
4. The congregation's appreciation of your work?	39	29.8	103	41.2
5. Possibility that you can make a significant contribution to the vitality and mission of that organization?	23	17.6	105	42.0
6. Your salary and living arrangements?	30	22.9	123	49.2
7. Members' willingness to carry out their Christian witness in the world?	7	5.3	23	9.2
8. The opportunity to exert creative leadership and try out new ideas?	37	28.2	100	40.0
9. The degree to which laymen share the leadership tasks of the church?	32	24.4	61	24.4
10. The degree to which the work utilizes your strengths rather than your weaknesses as a minister?	31	23.7	97	38.8

* Ratings of 5 or 6 on a six-point scale ranging from Very Dissatisfied (1) to Very Satisfied (6).

to study and be trained; and there was not a great deal more pleasure in the amount of time available for family and private life or in the degree to which laymen shared the leadership tasks of the church. Strong differences emerged, however, in satisfaction with the possibility of making a significant contribution to the vitality and mission of the church, the opportunity to exert creative leadership and try out new ideas, the salary and living arrangements, and whether the work utilized the minister's strengths rather than his weaknesses. From 38 to 50 percent of pastors showed high satisfaction with these four items, while only half as many ex-pastors did.

If the recital of information on task enjoyment and job satisfaction seems confusing, perhaps it can most easily be clarified in two sentences. First, ex-pastors and pastors seem to regard the same tasks as most enjoyable or least enjoyable— with the exception of community activity—and seem to be most satisfied and least satisfied with the same sorts of things. Second, however, ex-pastors enjoyed their work less and were more generally dissatisfied than pastors, with the chief area of difference being that pastors estimate more highly the opportunities and rewards of their work. In a word, the pastors seem to carry a kind of optimism about making a difference through their ministries, whereas ex-pastors show a depressed or hopeless attitude toward the work and its rewards. The significance of this difference for the making of career-change decisions is explored in chapter 5.

We rather expected ex-pastors to report a high degree of stress during their last church positions, presenting a marked contrast to the pastors' current level of stress. As Table B30 shows, however, the differences although present were not great. One ex-pastor out of 3 reported high stress, but so did 1 pastor out of 5. Two fifths of each group reported medium stress. Evidently the experience of stress in a job is nearly as typical of pastors as of ex-pastors.

We had suspected that ex-pastors would report being excluded from denominational or ecumenical leadership beyond the parish level. This could be an important source of alienation from peers, with consequent undermining of commitment to the ministry. In fact, we found no appreciable differences in either the types or levels of leadership involved in associations, conferences, and ecumenical groups. We concluded from this, that although the minister is an appallingly isolated practitioner, this is not because he lacks institutional leadership linkages. More subtle factors are involved, as chapter 4 explores in considerable detail.

How About Their Personal Lives?

The *marital status* of ex-pastors differs from that of the pastors in a very important way. (Table 3; details of marital status are found in Table B10.) Al-

Table 3. Marital Status of Ex-Pastors and Pastors

Marital Status	EX-PASTORS		PASTORS	
	Number	Percent	Number	Percent
Married and living with first wife	189	81.8	230	92.0
Separated or divorced	27	11.8	7	2.8
Widowed	4	1.7	8	3.2
Never married	7	3.0	5	2.0
No response	4	1.7	0	0
	231	100.0	250	100.0

though the vast majority of both groups are married and living with their first wives, nearly one eighth of the ex-pastors have been separated or divorced, whereas less than 3 percent of the pastors have. Although the total numbers are not large, the incidence of broken marriages reflects a highly significant factor in the decision to leave. This is discussed at length in chapter 5, where the marriage relationship is shown to carry heavy responsibility for supporting and guiding the minister's work. As for the size of families, there is no difference between the two groups (Table B11).

Ministers place a high emphasis on *education,* and it is no surprise that many of the men in our sample took additional training beyond seminary. It *is* surprising to discover, however, that ex-pastors have had substantially more higher education than pastors, 70 receiving master's degrees and 22, doctorates, as over against 35 master's degrees and 12 doctorates among pastors (Table B12). Approximately equal numbers of both groups took additional work in theological schools, but the proportion of ex-pastors working in public or private universities was more than three times that of pastors. In all, 114 ex-pastors reported education beyond the seminary, compared to 59 pastors. It is not surprising that the two groups differ sharply in fields pursued. Pastors went more heavily for religion, then for humanities (including history). Ex-pastors emphasized these two fields, too, but substantial portions also worked in social science, social work, education, and counseling (Table B13).

It does not appear to be the poorly educated who are moving from church ministries to secular work. Indeed, it is a truism that education is a facilitator of career advancement, and the same may well be equally true of career *change.*

The belief is widespread that loss or change of *personal faith* is responsible for many moves into secular employment. Our evidence, summarized and discussed in chapter 5, leads us to answer Yes and No to that proposition. *Yes,* important changes have been taking place in recent years in the theological views of ministers, and they are related to moves out of church employment. The changes are generally toward more liberal views, more tolerance for theological pluralism, and less interest in systematic theology (Tables 37–38 and pages 103–4). These changes have facilitated the redefinition of vocation to include secular ministries of many kinds.

On the other hand, with a few isolated exceptions, loss of faith does not seem to have driven men from the ministry. There is considerable evidence of revitalized faith after leaving church employment, as though the pastorate exerted a depressive effect on some. For many this renewal provided the basis for reconceiving themselves as ministers and their secular work as ministry. There is also much evidence that the changes observed among ex-pastors are occurring among pastors, although the latter adduce different causes. Our own and others' data reveal the massive changes occurring in Christian faith today and how the resulting climate creates a whole new view of church, ministry, and vocation.

Is Age a Factor?

Half of our ex-pastors have been out of church employment less than 3 years, and three fourths less than 5 years. About 1 in 20 has been out 15 years or more (Table B14). The differences in elapsed time since the move into secular employment raise a question about meaningful age comparisons. Should we compare the ages of ex-pastors when they moved, with pastors when *they* last moved or with pastors now? Most of our data were gathered with the latter comparison in mind: ex-pastors discussing their last church position and the decision to leave it, and pastors reporting on their current situation. This tells us in what ways pastors today resemble or differ from ex-pastors when they were deciding to leave church ministries. On the other hand, comparing the two groups at the time when they last moved gives us some idea of how the age distribution of men leaving compared with that of men staying but moving to another pastorate.

In Table 4 we have included a summary of both types of comparison (detailed comparisons are in Table B15). Ex-pastors and pastors did not differ greatly in age when leaving their last church positions: half of each group was under 38 and half over. The ex-pastors were more clustered in the middle-age group from 35 to 49 years old, but 1 in 8 was 50 or over. When one considers the personal and career significance of such a move, it seems remarkable that nearly two thirds of the ministers who left for secular employment did so *after* age 35 when family expenses are heaviest, career advancement possibilities highest, when pension credits have finally begun to amount to something, and when they are at an age where it is difficult to obtain placement and training in another occupation. The difficulty of such a move is underlined by the fact that those who left in their 40's and 50's tended more often to report financial loss in their change than those who left in their 20's and 30's. The latter were more likely to show financial gains by the move (Table B16).

It has been, on the average, five years since the pastors' last moves, which makes their median age nearly five years greater than that of the ex-pastors at the time of their moves. If we assume that the age distribution of UCC ministers has remained constant over the years, then it appears that moves out of church employment occur considerably more often among younger men than older men. For example, men under 35 comprise only 20.8 percent of pastors today but 34.6 percent of the ex-pastors at the time they left. The detailed breakdown in Table B15 shows that each age-group up to age 49 is overrepresented among ex-pastors, and each age-group over 50 is underrepresented. It is important to note, however, that the differences exceed 5 percent only *under* 30 and *over* 55. That is, the age distribution of pastors between 30 and 55 is about the same as that of ex-pastors in the same age range. Apparently the influences leading men out of church employment, while particularly strong in the 20's and weak after 55, operate with approximately equal force throughout the middle years of a minister's career.

Table 4. Age-Groups of Ex-Pastors and Pastors

Age-Group	Ex-Pastors (231) When Left Last Church Position	Pastors When Left Last Church Position	Pastors (250) Now
34 and under	34.6	36.4	20.8
35–49	49.9	39.6	42.0
50 and over	12.1	18.4	35.6
No response	3.4	5.6	1.6
	100.0	100.0	100.0
Median Age	38.9 yrs.	38.2 yrs.	43.4 yrs.

Were Their Careers Different?

As explained in chapter 2, we include both parish and nonparish ministers in the terms pastor and ex-pastor, since it is convenient to do so even though not strictly accurate. Actually, of every 20 ex-pastors, 15 held pastorates before leaving; 3 were associates, assistants, or other parish staff; 1 exercised a nonparish ministry; and the remaining 1 we are not certain about (Table B17). A comparable portion of pastors (15 out of 20) now hold pastorates, 1 out of 20 is a member of a parish staff, and 3 out of 20 are nonparish ministers. Recent figures from the UCC Council for Church and Ministry show that during 1968 approximately 70 precent of UCC clergy were in parishes. Since over 90 percent of our ex-pastors were in parishes, we suspect that moves into secular employment are occurring in disproportionate numbers from the parish rather than from nonparish ministries.

Another fact of interest is that more than twice as many ex-pastors as pastors have had interrupted careers, in which they previously left church employment for secular work and then returned (Table 41, page 113). On the other hand, pastors were more likely to have had continuous ministries uninterrupted by secular positions. It makes intuitive sense that people who have had prior experience in secular employment will more readily move out of church employment, but this is not quite accurate. Practically the same proportion—one fourth—of the careers of ex-pastors and pastors began with full-time secular work, so that just being a "delayed vocation" apparently does not increase the probability of moving out later. It is rather the experience of interruption which seems more influential. This is discussed further at the end of chapter 5.

Pastors now in service have had considerably longer ministerial careers than ex-pastors.* The median pastor career is 16.8 years with an average of 3.8 positions (Tables 5–6). Ex-pastors, on the other hand, served fewer years (median 10.7) and held a median of 3.5 positions. If our sample of pastors is representative of the UCC ministry today, it is plain that most of them (65.2%) have moved beyond the first 12 years of their careers, the same period during which nearly two thirds of the ex-pastors moved into secular employment. It is not surprising that the longer a man remains in church employment, the less likely it is that he will leave; what *is* surprising is that this effect of career stability only takes hold after the thirteenth year and does not become pronounced until the sixteenth year. In other words, we would expect ex-pastors to show a higher proportion of brief careers than pastors, but apparently, "brief" means 12 years or less. Moreover, a third of the ex-pastors served 13 years or longer. It is clear that these ministers were not shoots sprung up on rocky ground, withering in the summer sun's first heat. Many of them had roots in the ministry, persisting over a long enough time to have invested much of themselves in the church and to have a very clear understanding of what they were leaving.

---

* Data in this section refer only to ministerial positions for both ex-pastors and pastors. Secular positions have been excluded from these tabulations.

Table 6 shows, however, that a sixth of the ex-pastors served only one pastorate before leaving, while only a twentieth of the pastors have had such brief careers. Apparently there is an important group of ex-pastors who had very short careers in the ministry. If one discounts them for the moment and looks at ex-pastors and pastors who have held two or more positions, the distribution of both groups among the numbers of positions held is very similar. That is, if one subtracts the men who have held extremely short careers, there seems to be no important dif-

Table 5. Length of Ministerial Career

Years in Ministry	Percent of Ex-Pastors (216)	Percent of Pastors (248)
3 or less	9.7	1.6
4–6	20.3	8.0
7–9	16.2	10.8
10–12	17.1	12.8
13–15	12.0	14.0
16–21	12.5	18.0
22–27	6.0	11.2
28 or more	3.2	22.0
No response	2.8	1.6
	99.8	100.0
Median Years in Ministry	10.7 yrs.	16.8 yrs.

Table 6. Number of Ministerial Positions Held

Number of Ministerial Positions Held	Ex-Pastors		Pastors	
	Number	Percent	Number	Percent
1	20	16.7	13	5.4
2	25	20.8	56	23.2
3	28	23.3	64	26.6
4	18	15.0	40	16.6
5–6	20	16.7	51	21.2
7–8	6	5.0	15	6.2
9 or more	3	2.5	2	0.8
	120	100.0	241	100.0
Median Number of Positions	3.5		3.8	

ference in the rate of moving out at succeeding job-change points in the clergy-men's careers. This is consistent with our earlier observation that, discounting the very youngest and the very oldest, age makes little difference in the rate of movement out of ministerial work.

We calculated the mean length of ministerial position for each man's career. When these are tabulated, we find the average pastorate is more than a third longer for pastors than for ex-pastors, the median for the latter being 3.3 years, and for the former 4.6 years (Table 7). If then one tabulates the total number of one-year pastorates, two-year pastorates, and so on in the careers of these men, he finds that 46.6 percent of ex-pastors' positions were two years or less whereas only 29.4 percent of pastors' positions were two years or less (Table B18). As the jobs get longer, ex-pastors tend to have fewer of them, so that only 7.6 percent of ex-pastors' jobs were seven years or longer, while 18 percent of pastors' positions were.

These dry career statistics say important things about the experience of ex-pastors. We've already seen how earlier changes of denomination and experiences in secular jobs are associated more with the careers of ex-pastors than pastors. The more frequent job movement is further evidence that career patterns of change and interruption are characteristic of ex-pastors. The same finding emerged in a study of career change among United Presbyterian ministers, where brief pastorates were associated with a tendency to enter secular employment (Mills, 1969). Although the career length of ex-pastors indicates roots in the ministry, those roots rarely sank deeply into any one community. Short tenures would make it difficult for a man to establish himself and win the confidence of his people. Rapid movement may well be a symptom of underlying problems which erode the minister's occupational commitment and eventuate in his leaving church employment.

What Are They Doing Now?

The ministry is a varied occupation, with room for many types of persons and a variety of skills and interests. It is no wonder then that ex-pastors moved to many types of work. The field in which they are presently most frequently employed is social service or social change occupations (Table 8). Of the 39 in this field, approximately half (20) are in welfare administration of some type. The remainder are distributed among poverty programs, social work, community organization, youth organizations, and correctional and probation work. The second most popular field is education, where 11 of the 25 are in college administration, 6 in college teaching, 5 in secondary schools, and the remainder in specialized educational tasks.

The professions, arts, and sciences were chosen by 23 who constitute an extremely varied group: 7 in journalism and mass media, 6 in psychological counseling, 3 each in natural sciences and data processing, and the rest in an assortment of positions. The fourth general field, chosen by 17 ex-pastors, was business. Six men began their own consulting firms or other businesses, 4 each went into personnel and business sales, and the others are in business management. Of the

Table 7. Mean Length of Pastorate

| | EX–PASTORS | | PASTORS | |
MEAN LENGTH OF PASTORATE	NUMBER	PERCENT	NUMBER	PERCENT
0.1–1.9	13	10.7	6	2.5
2.0–2.9	36	29.8	29	12.1
3.0–3.9	35	28.9	39	16.2
4.0–4.9	17	14.0	43	17.9
5.0–6.9	13	10.7	73	30.4
7.0 and up	7	5.8	50	20.8
	121	99.9	240	99.9
MEDIAN	3.3 yrs.		4.6 yrs.	

Table 8. Current Employment of Ex-Pastors

	NUMBER	PERCENT
Education (nonreligious)	25	19.8
Social service or social change	39	30.9
Professions, arts, and sciences	23	18.2
Business fields	17	13.5
Labor, military, and other	17	13.5
Unknown	5	4.0
	126	99.9

remaining 17 for whom we have information, 6 are in state or city governmental positions, 4 are students, 6 are in blue-collar labor jobs, and 1 is unemployed.

Two things about this distribution of current occupations are worth noting here. The first is that men frequently described their present work as an *extension* of their ministries, often enabling them to spend more time at what they felt was really important in the ministry than their pastorates did. Approximately half the men are in education and service occupations which are obviously related to the ministry, and many of those in professions, arts and sciences, and business also regard their jobs as consistent with their original calling to the ministry.

Second, more than half the ex-pastors report improvement in their financial circumstances after leaving (Table B19). Less than a fourth report loss due to the move. A comparison of their current salaries with what they were earning in their last ministerial positions * shows that the ex-pastors' median salary now is

* Respondents were instructed to include in their ministerial salary data on allowance for housing where applicable.

$9,667 per year, and when they left church employment it was $6,256 (Table B20). This represents an average gain of more than 50 percent. Remembering that ex-pastors have been out less than three years, on the average, this is an impressive gain. Nearly half (45%) now are making over $10,000, whereas in their last ministry job less than a tenth (7.4%) earned that much. As Table B21 shows, current salary for ex-pastors is nearly $1,500 greater than for pastors. By contrast, at the beginning of their ministries ex-pastors earned less than pastors (Table B21).

The Decision to Leave

In the next few pages we will summarize the ways in which ex-pastors describe their decisions to enter secular employment. Much of this material is explored in later chapters, particularly what we have learned about the whole church. Men leaving pastoral ministries are only the entry point for this study. What they and the pastors have told us reveals much about the church as an institution and about the ministry as an occupation. At this point, however, we simply want to "tell it like it is," as the ex-pastors have experienced it.

DOMINANT REASONS

Everyone knows that human decisions are overdetermined; that is, a life decision is never the result of just one influence, even though one might have been sufficient to cause the decision. But there are priorities among causes, and we thought it would be useful to identify in a tentative way the top priority influence on each ex-pastor's decision. These we called the dominant reasons, and they are reproduced in Table 9. Perhaps the most compelling thing about this list is that

Table 9. Dominant Reasons Why Ex-Pastors Left Church Employment

REASONS	NUMBER	PERCENT
Sense of personal and professional inadequacy	22	17.1
Unable to relocate when necessary	19	14.7
Problems of wife and children	17	13.2
Opportunity to put training and skills to fullest use	12	9.3
Personal illness or breakdown	11	8.5
Dissatisfaction with parish work	10	7.8
Lack of church's spiritual growth and relevance was stultifying	10	7.8
Divorce or separation	9	7.0
Money problems	8	6.2
More attractive job opportunity	7	5.4
Other reasons	4	3.1
	129	100.1

it is such a multiplicity of reasons, reflecting the pressures of role expectations, money, marital problems, frustrated leadership, health, and limited resources. *There is no overwhelming reason why men "leave the ministry."* The dynamics of career decisions are varied, and what we see in the ex-pastors is simply a fraction of a larger group who struggle with the same problems but who have different approaches to the resolution and management of these problems. If we were to go back and redo this whole study, it would almost certainly involve intensive interviews with pastors as well as ex-pastors, and a more systematic attempt to focus upon the multiple sources of career pressures and the wide variety of clergy responses to them, rather than narrowing down to one type of response—that of leaving the field.

The second strong impression from Table 9 is that revolutionaries seem distinctly in the minority. That is, those who pull up stakes to work in greener pastures because they are disillusioned or angry about the church's irrelevance would principally be found among reasons 4, 6, and 7, which together account for only one fourth of the total. In spite of the strong words of advice in chapter 1, most ex-pastors we interviewed were inclined to place as much upon themselves as upon the church the burdens of failure or inadequacy. If our argument occasionally suggests that the church is chiefly at fault, it is because we see system pressures at work which many clergy do not, and what to them seems principally to be their own inadequacy, our analysis reveals as a deck stacked against them.

The fact that the ministry is an extremely demanding job is reflected in the primacy of reason 1, a sense of personal and professional inadequacy, as well as in the incidence of personal illness or breakdown. At the same time, the mobility problem is highlighted by reason 2, the inability of 19 men to relocate when it became necessary. There are many reasons why they have trouble relocating, some of which would justify their moves into secular work. But the placement problem, and the hostility which it engenders between its victims and the denominational representative who must try to help them, is very plain in the interview. The significance of family problems is also evident in items 3 and 8, also money problems in item 9. These will be discussed at length later. Finally, it is important to recall that not all reasons for moving are "push" reasons but that some men leave because they are attracted to work which is more rewarding or uses their training and skills more fully. Items 4 and 10 suggest such reasons.

Ex-pastors completed a questionnaire asking them to rate 24 reasons for making a move (Table B22). The fact that no reason received a high rating from as many as half the men reflects the diversity of "dominant reasons" in Table 9. However, three reasons were rated of high importance by a fourth or more of the ex-pastors and thus constitute concerns shared by many:

1. Disillusioned with the church's relevance to problems of modern world   43.5%
2. Opportunity arose to do specialized work or training   38.9%
3. Very attractive type of work offered   32.8%

Reasons that were most frequently listed as "not important at all" were:

1. Change coerced by denominational leadership   82.4%
2. Health problems made a change necessary   81.7%
3. More desirable region or community   79.4%

Money is often thought to be a major reason why men leave the ministry (Table B23). Based on the interviews, we concluded that money was "very much a factor" in only one decision in eight, that it was a moderate or small factor in as many more, but that in more than half the cases money really had nothing to do with the decision. It must be remembered here that dissatisfaction is only a genuine stimulus for career change when it changes to frustration; that is, when one begins to lose hope that he can correct the causes of this dissatisfaction. Inadequate salaries cause considerable distress in the ministry and are an important part of decisions of some men to leave. We heard some poignant stories about medical and other bills leading to hopeless indebtedness on marginal salaries. But we are convinced that few men leave church employment primarily for financial reasons. More about that in the following two chapters.

WHY DIDN'T THEY STAY?

In a way, the discussion of reasons for leaving also answers this question about why ex-pastors didn't *stay* in church ministries. But it is useful to approach the subject from a different angle. This is what we had in mind when, in the interview, we asked each man, "What would have had to be different for you to have remained in church employment?" The answers to this are analyzed in some detail in chapter 4, but briefly there were four types of response (Table B24):

1. If the church were different . . .
   —if church had moved toward a new or more relevant ministry   25
   —if either the minister's role or my personality were different   16
2. If more appropriate job had appeared . . .
   —if I had gotten a job to fit my interests or abilities   17
   —if I had been able to get a job immediately   17
   —if the job had been more satisfying   8
   —if the offer of another job had *not* come   3
3. If the circumstantial pressures on me had been different . . .
   —if I had had more money or better living conditions   10
   —if I had had time to rethink or renew my vocation   6
   —if I had remained married   5
   —if I had not felt compelled to resign   3
4. I would *not* have stayed.   8

It is plain again how varied are the responses of ex-pastors, reflecting the diverse origins of their decisions to move.

We need not stop with this diversity, however, for there are underlying similarities and themes that run through all the cases. These were revealed in a striking manner by a series of three questions answered by both pastors and ex-pastors (Tables B25–B26). The responses show that the professional peers from whom one would expect considerable support and strength during a difficult ministry were in fact often inaccessible to the ministers (Table B26). Moreover, UCC pastors and ex-pastors are very similar in reporting not only nonsupport from their peers but also their own distrust of other clergy and the devaluing of their praise (Table B25). At the same time, nonprofessional persons such as wife and close friends are rated extremely high both in the minister's desire for their approval and in the supportive function they perform. The implications of this complex issue are explored in detail in the next two chapters. We can summarize the findings, however, simply by noting that ex-pastors left church employment partly because the professional support structures that would have bound them more effectively into the occupation were nonsupportive, whereas the really effective support structures were extra-professional, helping during a tough time but not capable of strengthening occupational commitment. The similarity of pastors' and ex-pastors' views on this point is alarming.

When one puts all this together with the changing emphases in faith already reported, the growing accessibility of mission-type jobs outside the church, the accumulated pressures reflected in the "dominant reasons," and the tendency of local congregations to place maintenance above mission, we have a convincing answer to the question, Why didn't they stay?

Before leaving this topic, however, we want to point out that the ministry is not, either to ex-pastors or to pastors, a bundle of miseries or a vocational hair shirt—there are, of course, a few exceptions. Most regard the ministry as a worthy challenge with exciting possibilities and supremely important goals. Our point in detailing the reasons for leaving is not to tell sob stories about clergymen but to show that as an occupation within a major social institution there are system pressures and culture-wide trends which are reshaping the entire concept of ministry and the institutional patterns it will follow in the future. It is possible to see beyond the idiosyncratic accounts of each ex-pastor to the structural implications for the whole church. This is the most important level at which we have tried in this volume to answer the question, Why didn't they stay?

WHAT DIFFERENCE DID LEAVING MAKE IN THEIR LIVES?

This is a question we put directly to ex-pastors at the beginning of the interview. Most of their responses, relating to job satisfaction, relationships with others, feelings about themselves, marriage and family, personal faith and other areas, were positive: being out of church employment has left them freer, less pressured, more relaxed, more sure of themselves; in a word, for many of them it has been a new beginning, with renewing effects. Examples of these effects are the impact of the change on personal self-image, family problems, and financial circumstances.

Twenty ex-pastors consider themselves more free as persons now, 28 more confident or more adequate, and 12 spoke of generally improved feelings about themselves (Table B27). Similarly, 32 described family problems which have improved since leaving, and another 36 report that family problems were not a cause of leaving but the family is happier now (Table B28). Also 72 report improvement in their financial circumstances (Table B19).

On the other hand, there is an important minority for whom the move out of the pastoral ministry has not been so positive an experience. Twenty-five men describe themselves as troubled, feeling worse about themselves than before. For 7, their families are unhappier now, and another 14 were unable to save their marriages by leaving. Thirty-one experienced financial loss in leaving, although several of these have since regained or surpassed their former income level. And for another group, feelings about self, marital and financial circumstances, have not changed appreciably through the transition.

There is, therefore, no basis for euphoria about the joys of moving out of the pastorate, since for some the difficulty did not end with the move but has deepened since then. Nevertheless, a substantial majority found release and renewal in the experience of leaving church employment.

WILL THEY RETURN?

We began this chapter by reporting how few ex-pastors regard themselves as having "left the ministry" and how few pastors regard themselves as "permanently committed to the pastorate." This suggests a broad flexibility in the futures of both groups. Two questionnaire items asked how ex-pastors would feel about returning at some future time to the parish ministry or to some nonparish ministry (Table 10). Their responses confirm a large measure of openness to future ministry, but the caution of men who have learned painful lessons is also evident. Thirteen ex-pastors are eager to return to parish ministries and another 13 would be equally happy there as in their present work. Fifty-seven are open to call under some conditions but prefer not to return to the parish. Here, then, are 83 men representing varying degrees of openness to the pastorate in the future, with

Table 10. Ex-Pastors' Interest in Returning to the Church
Ministry at Some Future Time

	TO PARISH MINISTRY		TO NONPARISH MINISTRY	
	NUMBER	PERCENT	NUMBER	PERCENT
Eager to do so	13	9.9	20	15.3
Would be equally happy there as in present work	13	9.9	41	31.3
Is open to call under some conditions but prefers not to	57	43.5	34	26.0
Definitely prefers not to	39	29.8	20	15.3
No response	9	6.9	16	12.2
	131	100.0	131	100.1

another 39 definitely not willing to return. A series of cross-tabulations suggests that the eager ones are principally those who felt forced out by crises of various types: money, marital problems, or inability to relocate. They are not the men who report questioning their vocation, feeling inadequate or hopeless, frustrated by the work, or drawn by attractive secular jobs. By contrast, the men who definitely prefer not to return are those who were frustrated by the job, who would only have stayed had the role been differently defined, who did not enjoy the work and found the support system least supportive, whose wives were eager to leave and at the same time were warm and supportive of their husbands, for whom money was not much of a factor and who were attracted by interesting secular work.

Men open to call under some conditions are more likely the second group just described than the first, reporting considerable frustration at the lack of relevance and vigor in the church, questioning their own vocations, feeling hopeless about improving the church, and responding to a chance to do specialized or interesting work outside.

This suggests a distinction between chronic and acute problems leading to moves into secular work. The chronic problems are those related to job frustration, hopelessness, vocational doubts, and a nonsupportive system. These accumulate over time, and those who leave because of such chronic distress show only the most guarded interest in returning to the parish. On the other hand, the moves of some men are precipitated by acute problems related to money, family, placement difficulties, etc. These men tend to be much more interested in returning. Based on this reasoning, an important need in the church's support structures is for acceptable short-term aid to help ministers and their families manage sudden crises, and to relocate and begin again when the situation stabilizes. One of the most frequent feelings we have encountered among ex-pastors of many denominations is the sense of being abandoned at a point of critical need. Our data make it clear that such needs were largely responsible for the departure of some men who now are quite interested in returning. The church has little capability for helping them back in.

Looking again at Table 10, nearly half the ex-pastors are eager to reenter non-parish ministries or would be equally happy there as in their present work. Only 20 men definitely reject it as a possibility. Although the numbers are different, cross-tabulations show the same general pattern of acute problems and high urgency in leaving among ex-pastors who are now interested in returning, and chronic problems and less urgency among those who now are not interested.

In reading the responses of ex-pastors to this question and to an interview item covering the same topic, we were struck by the frequency with which respondents want to minister. The circumstances of the interview—sponsored by a church board, usually in a church-related facility, and dealing with questions of ministry—may have created a certain halo effect around the discussion of self-image and future work. But the pattern was too consistent to be dismissed so easily as an artifact. In the last analysis, we were talking to ministers. Ex-pastors, but—with few exceptions—not ex-ministers. One of those exceptions exhorted his fellow conferees to give up being frauds, to stop kidding themselves about the ministry, and to accept the fact that they are now out of it. Instead of causing an electric confrontation, this fiery speech simply drowned in a sea of ministerial concern. There were indeed polarizations in the conferences: between those who want to work within the denomination and those who want to operate independently, between those who want to renew the local church and those who feel it is beyond all help, and between those who want confrontation with denominational leaders whom they distrust and those who want to give help and support to present leadership. But there was a broad, unspoken consensus that ministry—in some form, somewhere—is the raison d'être of life and work.

Our conclusion is that whether or not most of these men remain in secular employment or return to the church ministries, the encounters with them and the data of this study thoroughly confirm that most of them are still "hooked" on the institution and represent a major pool of leadership talent.

ARE THE WOMEN DIFFERENT FROM THE MEN?

The four women who attended the conferences and were interviewed constitute a very different group from the men. Although the confidential nature of the data forbids detailed discussion, some general comments will convey the flavor of their responses. All four are single, and three are now graduate students working toward master's or doctoral degrees. Three regard the problems of being a woman professional as central to their reasons for leaving church employment.

The problem of being a woman professional in the church is described in several ways by these three:

No one wants me on a team.

• • •

I'm not welcome at ministers' meetings.

• • •

What do we do with a woman minister or any member of a minority group?

• • •

Single men also have a hard time.

• • •

I haven't advanced to the degree that I should. I'll be on this level forever.

• • •

You do all the dirty work as a woman in mission work.

• • •

You can't be a professional woman in the church. I want to be a professional woman.

• • •

The best woman ministers are extraordinarily free of self-consciousness.

• • •

I never learned to knuckle under to the male ego.

• • •

Being a woman has certain advantages—people are politer—but there are disadvantages: a single woman needs a full-time salary.

• • •

Since I am a woman, I've never had a clear vision of the route my career in the church would take. A "pastoral ministry" never seemed likely or desirable.

The fourth woman ex-pastor moved because she felt the need of more training in educational and group skills, although an important subordinate theme was conflict with colleagues on the church staff. Throughout three of the four interviews the difficulty of relocating when one needs to was mentioned. The sluggish placement procedures of the UCC seem to affect women even more than men.

Three of the women were seminary graduates. They ranged in age from 39 to 55 when they left church employment. Only 3 gave their job histories, totaling 6 secular and 19 ministerial positions. Of these, 15 were 2 years or less, and only 1 was as long as 5 years. Two positions were pastorates, 5 were assistant pastorates, and the remaining 12 ministerial positions were staff jobs in Christian education and related fields. Only 4 jobs reached the $8,000 salary bracket, 4 were between $6,000 and $7,999, and the others were less. All 4 women report a drop in income since leaving, due partly to the student status of three. Highly mobile and interrupted careers with limited responsibilities and salaries thus characterize the women ex-pastors.

In both job satisfaction and task enjoyment the responses are not unlike those of the male ex-pastors, except in two respects: (1) the restricted job descriptions of the women made more of the listed tasks "irrelevant"; (2) "freedom to preach and act as you see fit," rated high by many of the men, was highly satisfying to only one woman. The tasks the women most highly enjoyed were preaching, teaching adults, and conducting committee and board meetings. Men ex-pastors agree with the first two but rarely enjoyed the meetings. The women did not highly enjoy general calling or programming church group activity, thus agreeing with the men; they also did not enjoy serious study and writing or community leadership, activities which the men did highly enjoy.

On the whole, there were no serious family complications or faith changes reported. Two have had serious emotional problems, the effects of which still trouble them. Three of the women are rather skittish about returning to the parish ministry, while the fourth would like to return to Christian education work in the parish. Two plan to reenter nonparish ministries, and a third would like to.

Three women responded to the pastor's questionnaire. One is a stalwart religious education worker, unmarried and "eighty years young," now ministering to older adults on a part-time basis. Her profile of satisfaction, task enjoyment, friendships, and theological changes is more similar to that of male pastors than to that of women ex-pastors. A second pastor has a 35-year history of small town pastorates, is unmarried, and differs from men pastors only in the *extremely* low ratings she gives to clergy peers and denominational executives as part of the support system. These two women did not complete seminary.

The third is quite young, married to a minister, and expecting soon to enter a secular field for which she has prepared herself. She is a seminary graduate and has worked both in Christian education and in secular education since her marriage. She differs from the others in showing no extremes of role satisfaction or enjoyment—rather, a series of middle ratings—and in reporting growing uncertainty of faith and disinterest in theology. She also regards fellow clergy and denominational executives as unsupportive and highly isolating. Salary and interprofessional communication seem to have been serious problems for her. In many ways she resembles men ex-pastors more than any other group.

Our sample of seven women is too small for valid generalizations. The ex-pastors' careers clearly are different from those of their male counterparts, but the women pastors do not seem very different from the men. We can't tell whether the ex-pastors' anger at the problems of being a woman professional is more a cause or an effect of their moves out, but both are true to some extent. In any case it is a major distinction between the four ex-pastors and the three pastors.

Fitting It All Together

Even at its best, research invariably produces a combination of satisfaction and frustration in those who interpret the findings. As with other projects, ours has produced a core of clarity and a fuzzy fringe. Having tried to let the data speak for themselves in this chapter, we have adapted existing theories of organization and decision-making to interpret these data in the next two chapters. Since there is no attempt at any other point in the book to state in summary fashion the principal findings of the research, this chapter concludes with a series of propositions drawing together the conclusions of chapters 3–5. We will leave it to the reader to integrate the advice of chapter 1 with the findings summarized here. Our own efforts to do so constitute the policy implications of chapter 6.

First, however, the matter of the "dropout rate" can no longer be avoided. We have no data by which an accurate rate can be calculated for the UCC, although having 370 names and knowing that 74 percent of our respondents had left in the past 5 years, we can estimate that 274 departures occurred in 1963–68, or about 55 per year. Our 5 percent sample of men currently in church positions produced 20 responses from men now in secular work, 14 of whom were not in our ex-pastor sampling list. Multiplying the 14 by 20 (the sampling fraction), this means that as many as 280 more have left, 74 percent of which would be 207, representing the 1963–68 period. If, then, we *double* our original estimate (which almost certainly overestimates the number we missed), the total is still only 110 per year, or slightly over 1 percent of the active UCC clergy in 1968.

Most occupational groups would regard a 1 percent annual leakage as a vast improvement and probably a salutary influence on the group. Figures released by Jack McLeod (1969), quoting William H. Henderson, about the "so-called minister shortage" not only show a minister surplus among United Presbyterians but an alarmingly low dropout rate: "In the past 6 years the largest number to be removed from office, by demission and all other reasons, was 60, in 1964. Out of the 13,000 active ministers, that's a very small proportion" (p. 11). Comparable statistics have been released by Episcopal authorities showing ordinations nearly doubling withdrawals for all reasons in 1960–65 (Pusey and Taylor, 1967). American Baptists have recently studied members leaving their retirement plan (Young, 1969). Of the 173 ministers who left in 1968, at least 33 remained in ministerial employment, leaving 140 entering secular employment or graduate study, or about 3 percent of retirement-plan members.

We could go on in this vein, but the main point is clear: among Protestant clergy the evidence points not to a drop-out crisis but to a mobility and morale crisis, a situation in which there are too many ministers for the congregations that can adequately support them, and in which sluggish placement breeds sinking morale. We may very well, if the situation continues this way, have a sharp increase in movement out of church ministries; but it is not now a reality. When and if it occurs, however, as our study plainly shows, it will be a *system crisis* through and through, and not simply the actions of disgruntled individuals.

Bearing in mind, therefore, that we are not studying a runaway epidemic but a persistent low-grade infection, what has our diagnostic examination of the symptoms told us about the health of the church and its prospects for the future?

1. Ex-pastors are not ex-ministers, nor are pastors permanently pastors. A broad understanding of vocation, which is marked by an intense desire for the ministry, exists among both groups. If sometimes that ministry is defined over against the institution, the gradual liberalization and pragmatization of theology makes it relatively easy to redefine ministry in secular terms. Ex-pastors have done so on a large scale, and the basic rationale is shared by many pastors.

2. In addition to sharing recent theological trends, ex-pastors and pastors are similar in racial, parental, and community background, and in age—except for the very youngest and oldest. In general, they enjoy the same role tasks most and least, and are satisfied most and least with the same aspects of ministry. They both regard peers and denominational executives with low esteem, and invest wives and nonpeer close friends with the major support and reference functions. Ex-pastors feel they were inadequately prepared by seminaries.

3. Ex-pastors have a stronger pattern of early changes than pastors in denomination, in career, and in jobs; they are better educated, more interested in community activities, and less in the core pastoral roles of preaching, calling, and helping individuals to commitment, less satisfied with the rewards and opportunities of the parish (including salary) and less hopeful about making a difference there. Ex-pastors are disproportionately more from pastorates, are more likely than pastors to be under 30 and less likely to be over 55, feel less support from laymen and desire it less, and have greater marital problems.

4. Ex-pastors left church employment for a variety of reasons, none of which accounts for a majority of the decisions. The reasons include personal crises, a sense of inadequacy, disillusionment and frustration with the church, inability to relocate when necessary, family problems, attractive work opportunities. Some problems are chronic, leading to low interest in returning to church ministry; other problems are acute, more often followed by a desire to return. Ex-pastors

earn more, are freer and more relaxed, and report improved financial and family situations. They found their jobs most often through system contacts, although a fourth made sudden, ill-prepared decisions. Most had contemplated leaving for a long time.

5. The church as an occupational system fails to meet the needs of its professionals adequately. Weaknesses in the training, hiring, work, rewards, and support systems are evident in the experience of ex-pastors. At the same time, new careers are opening in "mission" occupations such as social service, social change, and education; and the combined effects produce intense pressures outward from pastoral ministries.

6. The family bears special importance in clergy careers. Family welfare, wife's role satisfaction, and marital harmony are crucial determinants of career decisions. Few ministers seem to real. ze this fact.

7. Faith changes are marked in recent years, growing out of maturity and social involvement (ex-pastors) or pastoral involvement (pastors). Deepening commitment may still accompany loosening ties to institution and the radical redefinition of ministry. Loss of faith is not a major basis for career change.

8. Career-change decisions often have roots in years of deliberation but are precipitated by "tipping point" experiences which coincide with the eroded occupational commitment. The combined effect of system conflict and accumulated dissatisfaction shift the hope/frustration balance and begin the search for other kinds of work. Evidence that ex-pastors and pastors differ by being on opposite sides of the tipping point makes it essential to develop support structures to nurture hope and manage frustration.

4 / THE CHURCH AS AN OCCUPATIONAL SYSTEM

"What difference has it made in your life to be in secular work?" we asked the ex-pastors. We asked this question in an open-ended way and expected a wide variety of answers. When we looked at the first response each man gave, we found that a large majority of their answers fell into four categories. The responses appear in Table 11.

Table 11. Difference in Life Since Entering Secular Work

	NUMBER	PERCENT
The working conditions are better. We have more money, more security, more time for the family, better housing, etc.	27	21.4
Personal factors are better. I'm less tense, happier.	29	23.0
The new job is more satisfying, more fulfilling; I use more skills	28	22.2
There is a change in the role expected of me. Perfection is not expected. I'm more a human. People relate to me on a more realistic basis.	14	11.1
No difference in life	5	4.0
There is a lack in my life now	8	6.3
Not enough data	15	12.0
	126	100.0

When person after person feels happier, freer, more rewarded, more human, more secure, and more satisfied after he leaves an occupation, regardless of why he left, we begin to suspect some inherent strains within that occupational system.

Our suspicions, it turns out, are well grounded. We found people unhappy in a pastorate because they were not trained for the job they were doing, they could not relocate when the time came to move, they could not fulfill their conception of the Christian goals, they did not receive ample material rewards, they did not receive the support of fellow pastors or their denominational executives, there were extra strains on their families and their own personalities due to the job. If these complaints were true of only the ex-pastors we might possibly, if we were very establishment oriented, dismiss them as a bunch of "ne'er-do-wells" who shouldn't have been in the ministry in the first place. However, the same complaints were made by the pastors, which merely reinforces our hypothesis of inherent strains.

The hypothesis which will be pursued in this chapter is that the church as an occupational system has some structural elements which are contrary to the needs of the clergyman in following his professional career, his religious conscience, and his private life. The alternatives available to him seem to provide him a better opportunity on all levels.

It is quite difficult to study the organization of the church and its organizational relationship to individual clergymen. The total church organization, from local church to the highest national office, is intertwined with the life-span of the professional, from his early socialization to retirement. Many of the individual clergymen are both the products and the leaders of the organization. However, with ex-pastors we are studying people who have entered and subsequently left the occupation. Since they are currently separated from the church as an employer we are able to concentrate on the pastor as a professional aside from the church as an organization.

Since we identify the professional clergyman as an integral part of the church organization, Alvin Gouldner's examination of the relation of a system to its parts seems a useful approach to the problem (Gouldner, 1959, pp. 241 ff.). There are two characteristic aspects of a social system. One is that there are a number of parts which act interdependently with each other in a regular way. The other is that these parts tend to act in such a way as to keep the system stable or in equilibrium. We are especially interested in the problem of interdependence of system parts in this study.

In order to have interdependence between a system (the church) and its part (a clergyman), there must be functional reciprocity between them. That is, not only must the clergyman fill the manpower needs of the church, but the church must fill the occupational or professional needs of the clergyman. Reciprocity connotes that both have rights and duties. Reciprocity means that B, a system part, serves a function for A, a system, contingent on A's providing a function for B. If either the A or the B has a greater power, it may force the other or provide a function without reciprocity. If either A or B has still other sources which supply it with the services it needs, it is less dependent on the other and may not reciprocate.

Gouldner's theory is summarized by the three elements in the participation of a system part in a system: (1) the benefits that a system and its parts receive from each other, (2) the power that a system and its parts have over each other, and (3) alternative sources of services that each has.

The first element, that of mutual meeting of needs, will be discussed later. The second element, power, needs explication. In a formal organizational table of the

United Church of Christ, an individual clergyman has practically no power. He can either provide the services needed by the church in the way that the church wants, or he must leave. The clergyman as a professional feels that he has the right to do his job as he sees it, and strives for some power of his own.

The power of either the church to fully control or the clergyman to reach his own autonomy is dependent on the third element of Gouldner's system, alternative sources of services. If the church has many more clergymen than it has churches which need serving, when a deviate—in the church's eyes—comes along, the church can ignore him. If the clergyman who wants to serve has no alternative opportunities which will fit his own professional self-image, then he will serve according to the church's definition. In this case, the church has the power.

However, in more recent times, the power has evened because the clergyman has some alternative sources of service. For this to occur two important things happened, one in the system, the other outside of the system: 1. In the system the definition of minister changed in the seminaries, in colleges, in church literature. The working priest, specialized inner-city ministries, and new ministries are hailed as innovations in church literature. 2. Outside of the system alternative sources of service such as the Peace Corps, the Job Corps, social work, special education, etc. were increasingly visible. The clergyman today can see himself serving God and man in many different occupational areas.

The newly found power of the clergyman means that the church as a hiring organization must examine more closely the needs of the clergyman which it must meet in order to keep sufficient manpower. In the following sections, we will describe the organization of the United Church of Christ. We will then examine the occupational needs of a clergyman in terms of the efficacy of the system in supplying those needs.

The United Church of Christ

The United Church of Christ is a church system with several principal subsystems. Each subsystem has its own functions and could be considered a system of its own. The principal subsystems which are applicable in this study are: (1) the judicatories—local, state, and national; (2) the local congregation; and (3) the individual clergyman, the structures in the church that contribute to his professionalization, and his peer-group systems.

THE JUDICATORIES

The United Church of Christ has three levels of organization: the local association of churches, the state conference, and the national General Synod. Each of these organizations is an important subsystem of the church. Its functions are the coordination of activities and moneys of the system, the institution of new programs, the orientation and supervision of personnel, the setting of standards of performance, the allocation of rewards to the successful, the application of punishment to the deviants, and the setting of goals of the system. Each subsystem of the total organization has a formal organizational table with job description and job differentiation. Each subsystem has explicit formal goals and implicit organizational self-maintenance goals. Before proceeding, it is necessary to look at the dichotomy between these two sets of goals.

The major goal of the church is to make some change in the lives of people. On one level, this means changing individual lives in some way; renewing them, causing them to be reborn, educating them, giving hope, fellowship and care to them, etc. On another level, this means a corporate change—working for peace, justice, providing services such as food, clothing, child care, care for the aged, education, etc.

Both of these goals require organization and money to be most efficient and effective. Therefore, organizational and administrative goals are very necessary. The paradox within the church is obvious. The organizational structure is a vehicle for its primary goals. Maintaining the organization requires money, and its growth can be measured in quantitative terms such as membership statistics and contributions. However, the primary professional goals of the church are making a difference in individual or collective lives of people. These goals, which are practically impossible to measure, are the ones from which the clergyman derives his identity as a professional.

THE LOCAL CONGREGATION

Another major subsystem of the church is the local congregation. In the UCC, the local congregation is autonomous in terms of power and authority. It has the power because most of the money comes from the local church. If a local church chooses to withdraw from the UCC, it legally retains all its property to dispose of at will.

The local congregation is made of laymen, who are involved in other occupational systems. For many of them, the church is given only a secondary or marginal commitment as compared with family and occupational systems. They hire the professional with the best qualifications as judged by the standards with which they are familiar. These are usually secular standards, because they feel more comfortable with secular standards.

The goals of the subsystem of the local church may be quite different from those of either the professionals who staff the local association or state conference or the clergyman who is hired to lead the congregation. While they share some common values with the professionals, most of the laymen do not share the continued training into the profession which the clergy have. However, in the UCC, the local church has the task of supervising the professional in many aspects of his work and life. It can withhold the money and staff which the clergyman needs to do his work; it can fail to increase his salary or it can fire him.

THE CLERGYMAN

The clergyman is recruited, trained, and socialized into the profession by subsystems of the church. This means that not only does he learn the skills necessary to perform his job but he incorporates into his personality and total self, attitudes and values in keeping with the norms of the profession.

There are several subsystems in a church which contribute to the socialization process. First, the *recruitment system* influences the development of the self-image. The individual normally enters the system through the local church. Experiences such as the influence and personal interaction with clergymen and dedicated laymen in the church, success in youth-group activities, summer religious conferences, a personal religious experience, or a sensitivity to the needs of people create and reinforce the desire to become a clergyman. Often, strong social rewards from the decision, such as from family and other lay people, reinforce the decision even more.

It is seldom the conscious desire to become a leader in the organizational structure which attracts the young person into the church, but the ideal of making a difference in the lives of individuals either in terms of salvation or in terms of changing social conditions which will lead to a change in individual lives.

Moberg (1962, p. 484), in a study of 1,704 students from 57 seminaries, reports their chief reason for entering the ministry. Thirty-one percent felt a need of man and society for Christ. Twenty-six percent wanted to serve mankind. Thirty-eight percent felt a "call from God." Even the definition of "call" varied considerably, and in some cases included a call to service. In a preliminary study by this author 23 of the 29 clergymen interviewed in depth entered the ministry because of a desire to help people (Burch, 1969).

The second influence on the development of the professional self-image of the clergyman is *seminary*. Once the choice has been made, the young recruit must spend three or more years in a seminary for training following his college education. Seminaries are seldom dependent on local churches for financial resources. Therefore, they are less open to feedback from the local church as to training needs. The socialization process which is carried on in seminary has a profound effect on the self-image of the professional. To the degree that seminaries control entry to the profession, they can control the personality standards as well as the scholastic standards of the profession. During training, a seminarian is provided with a new language, and a reference group and training in understanding the doctrine, the faith, and his role. By far the major part of his time is spent in learning the professional role of preacher, teacher, priest, pastor, and prophet. Few of the requirements of seminaries have anything to do with the practical concerns of organization, administration, time allocation, community power structure, use of volunteers, change strategies, conflict management, etc.

Professional peers are a third influence on the young clergyman's self-image. In his training years, his peers reinforced his own idea of the professional role. In his recruitment he was swayed by social and religious ideals. In his training, intellectual ideals were added. His seminary professors as well as his fellow students reinforced idealism, altruism, intellectualism, and theological purity.

Let us again mention the three elements of participation in a social system: (1) the benefits that a system and its parts receive from each other, (2) the power that a system and its parts have over each other, (3) alternative sources of services that each has.

As long as a church has power over the clergyman, it can force him to produce without meeting his needs. This power is based on (a) supply and demand in the system and (b) alternative jobs that a clergyman can take outside the system. As the available alternatives increase, the power of the church to demand service without giving benefits to the clergyman decreases.

Until recently, the number of clergymen who took secular jobs did not particularly bother church leaders. There remained sufficient young clergymen to fill the available churches. However, some of the more insightful leaders see that the men who are leaving may be a harbinger of the future. They are trying to tell the organization something. The fact that the ex-pastors seem very similar in most ways to the pastors is an indication of the seriousness of the problem.

It is our contention that the UCC in the past has failed at many points to reciprocate or meet the employment needs of the professional clergyman. These clergymen have been recruited, trained, and socialized as professionals. They enter the occupational system of the church to meet its manpower needs. However, the system must meet their needs also. The occupational needs of the clergyman are:

1. A training system that adequately prepares him for the work.

2. A hiring system that facilitates getting a job, changing jobs, and progressing in his career.

3. A work system that provides an opportunity to do work which is satisfying and self-fulfilling.

4. A reward system that brings satisfactory rewards—both explicit monetary rewards and implicit social rewards.

5. A support system that provides him with professional support against the vagaries of a hiring organization which might exploit him.

In the following section, we will look at how the United Church of Christ met the occupational needs of the pastors who left.

The Occupational Needs of Clergymen

TRAINING

We asked the ex-pastors an open-ended question during the course of the interview: Do you now think that you were well prepared for the ministry at ordination? The amount of congruence in the responses was surprising. Less than one third of the clergymen, or 36, considered themselves well prepared for their ministry. Of the remainder, 34 blamed their unpreparedness on the lack of practical concerns taught in seminary. Another 20 felt that the seminaries had not prepared them spiritually or emotionally for the role the church expects the clergyman to play. Another 19 said unqualifiedly that they were poorly prepared. A final 9 gave no response.

It may be that a feeling of inadequacy causes a person to blame his seminary for poor preparation. We examined the two questions together. Ex-pastors were asked in the questionnaire how important was a feeling of personal inadequacy in the decision to leave. The results are reported in Table 12. There was very little

Table 12. Adequacy of Preparation for the Ministry and
Personal Inadequacy as a Cause for Leaving

PREPARATION	IMPORTANCE OF PERSONAL INADEQUACY AS A CAUSE				
	NONE	LOW	MEDIUM	HIGH	TOTAL
Well prepared	16	10	5	5	36
Not practically	11	11	4	8	34
Not spiritually or emotionally as needed	19	4	4	5	32
Poorly prepared	5	5	4	5	19
	51	30	17	23	121

association between feelings of personal inadequacy and adequacy of preparation for the ministry. The ex-pastors felt poorly prepared professionally regardless of feelings of personal inadequacy.

It may be that a person feels poorly prepared in proportion to his expectations. Therefore we looked at the response to another question, together with the question on preparedness. The ex-pastors were asked, When you went to seminary, were you primarily: (*check one*)

1. Seeking a faith?
2. Already a believer, and seeking a vocation?
3. Already clear about your vocation, and seeking to prepare for it?
4. Other (*write in*).

We would expect those seeking a faith to need not only practical skills and intense socialization but also an intangible, unmeasurable element of faith. Those seeking a vocation would require more socialization—i.e., spiritual-emotional support—and those seeking preparation would look for the practical skills. The responses for all ex-pastors are tabulated in Table B29; for those interviewed, the cross-tabulation data are given below in Table 13. Here we find the expected differences across categories. All 12 of those who entered seminary looking for a faith feel poorly prepared in some way. Twenty-one of those looking for preparation found seminary training not practical. Twelve who sought a vocation found they were not trained spiritually or emotionally to deal with the parish. These are statistically significant numbers.

To a large extent, ex-pastors consider their training to have been faulty. Some of their remarks illustrate the feeling:

> Seminaries are heavy with theory and abstraction. I was pumped up with theology and Bible study.

> •   •   •

> Seminary education is about as far removed from church work as I can imagine. The faculty was old, without anything new and fresh. I had

to work that out in the church. There was no help to understand church administration. Not much help in preaching or help in relating to people was given. The seminary is a closed community; the faculty are out of touch with the life of the church and with laymen.

The training system prepares our professionals to be concerned with people, church-affiliated or not. It teaches them to be priests and prophets and scholars. The church, however, needs administrators, organizers, committee workers, money raisers, power manipulators as well. The goals of the training and the needs of the church seem to be so incongruent that strain in the system is inherent in terms of role expectations of the clergyman.

Table 13. Adequacy of Preparation for Ministry and Purpose of Seminary

	PURPOSE OF SEMINARY				
PREPARATION	FAITH	VOCATION	PREPARATION	OTHER	TOTAL
Well prepared	0	10	23	2	35
Not practically	5	3	21	2	31
Not spiritually or emotionally as needed	4	12	13	2	31
Poorly prepared	3	6	10	0	19
	12	31	67	6	116

HIRING

In the UCC, each individual clergyman is a free agent. When he feels the time has come to change jobs, he has several options open to him. He can write to the national office with information to bring his dossier up to date. He informs the office and when inquiries come in from local churches needing clergymen, his dossier along with others is sent to the local church. The local church has the final say on whom it hires. The clergyman can also let his friends all over the country know that he is looking for a job. They can recommend him to churches in their area with openings. Usually the process is a long and tedious one. Several churches might be considering the same candidate for six to eight months and all decide on other candidates.

If there is any urgency in the current situation—that is, if the clergyman must move quickly—he often looks at secular jobs which àre available to him. When the new pastorate does not appear in time, he may well take one of those secular jobs.

Two questions that we asked both the ex-pastors and the pastors illustrate the problem involved in this slow process. First, we asked, Which one of the following best describes the urgency of your situation when you left church employment? *

1. Had no choice—could not have stayed in the ministry any longer.
2. Could have stayed in the ministry but had to leave that position immediately.
3. Could have stayed in that position awhile longer but not indefinitely.
4. Could have stayed in that position indefinitely.

The responses are noted in Table 14. (The first choice was not included in the

Table 14. Urgency of Leaving Last Position

DEGREE OF URGENCY	EX–PASTORS		PASTORS	
	NUMBER	PERCENT	NUMBER	PERCENT
Had to leave ministry immediately	16	12.2	Not included	
Had to leave job immediately	17	13.0	29	11.6
Could stay less than a year	16	12.2	23	9.2
Could stay a year or more	25	19.1	78	31.2
Could stay indefinitely	45	34.4	109	43.6
No response	12	9.2	11	4.4
	131	100.1	250	100.0

pastor's questionnaire.) Thirty-seven percent of the ex-pastors and 20 percent of the pastors could have stayed in their last position less than a year. United Church of Christ executives acknowledge that the job-hunting process usually takes longer than a year. The problem is evident.

Both groups were next asked the cause of the urgency expressed above. They were given the following choices.

1. Due chiefly to your own feelings?
2. Due chiefly to the pressure of others to get you out?
3. Due chiefly to family problems?
4. Other (*write in*).

If a local church is pressuring a man to leave, or if his marriage is in trouble or his children need a change, it is untenable for him to remain in the situation long enough to go through the regular job-finding channels. In cross-tabulating these two responses we see the number for whom outside pressure made an immediate move necessary. Table 15 shows the results for the ex-pastors.

Twenty-five of the 95, or more than one quarter (see box in table), had outside pressures from family or others to move in less time than the system takes. One ex-pastor said, "I had no intention of leaving the ministry, but only to change

---

* The item as asked of pastors referred to "the urgency of your situation when you moved from your previous position to your present job." Since response 1 was not applicable to pastors, it was omitted.

Table 15. Urgency of Leaving Last Position and Cause of Urgency

	CAUSE OF URGENCY				
DEGREE OF URGENCY	OWN FEELINGS	OTHERS	FAMILY	OTHER	TOTAL
Had to leave ministry immediately	5	4	3	2	14
Had to leave job immediately	3	7	2	5	17
Could stay less than a year	4	5	4	3	16
Could stay a year or more	16	2	0	5	23
Could stay indefinitely	8	0	1	16	25
	36	18	10	31	95

Table 16. Dominant Reasons for Leaving and "Would Have Stayed" Responses Pertaining to the Hiring System

	DOMINANT REASONS			
WOULD HAVE STAYED IF I COULD HAVE:	I NEEDED A JOB AND COULDN'T FIND ONE	OPPORTUNITY TO PUT TRAINING TO FULLEST USE	NEW JOB	TOTAL
Gotten a job immediately	6	0	2	8
Gotten a job to fit my interests	2	3	3	8
	8	3	5	16

churches. Several pulpit committees came to visit. After several months, I was offered a job at a Lions' Club meeting. The chief of the probation department was a member of the club and suggested I join his staff."

So far, we have been looking at the hiring system only in terms of finding a job. Another problem with this system is finding a job to fit the interests, training, specialties, or growing competence of the job-seeker. Over a period of years a mature person becomes aware of his strengths, his weaknesses, his talents, his special competences. When job hunting, he would like to find a job that takes advantage of his good points and minimizes his weak ones. The UCC does not take advantage of the specialties of its professionals. One ex-pastor explained it, "If something had been offered that was a challenge in another place, I would have taken it. The opportunities all involved a cut in salary." Another said, "I didn't really make a decision to leave, but an opportunity came along which offered another variety of service."

During the course of the interview we asked ex-pastors, What would have had to be different for you to have remained in church employment? As a reliability check, the coded answers were then cross-tabulated with the dominant reason for leaving the church as an occupational system. The pertinent results are in Table 16. Sixteen of the 131 ex-pastors left the church chiefly because of the breakdown in the hiring and job-changing mechanism. Other questions in the questionnaire indicate that many were dissatisfied with not being able to find jobs which fitted their needs.

The hiring system of the UCC is inadequate in helping a clergyman to relocate either quickly or effectively. A clergyman who is being pressured by his congregation to leave and has to wait six or eight months for various local churches to consider him, begins to look for nonchurch alternatives that he might take if his time runs out. In the course of his looking he is likely to find other jobs which will fit his professional self-image satisfactorily and in some cases extremely well.

WORK

We asked the ex-pastors to rate a series of statements as to their importance in the decision to leave the church. One of these statements was, Didn't enjoy the work of the pastorate. We cross-tabulated the responses to this statement with the responses to the statement, I would have stayed if . . . Table 17 shows the results.

Table 17. Didn't Enjoy Work as a Cause for Leaving, and Pertinent Responses to "Would Have Stayed If . . ."

	DEGREE OF IMPORTANCE OF "DIDN'T ENJOY WORK" AS CAUSE				
WOULD HAVE STAYED IF:	NONE	LOW	MEDIUM	HIGH	TOTAL
I could have gotten a job to fit my interests	6	7	3	4	20
The church was interested in a new kind of ministry	6	7	8	4	25
The role of the minister was defined differently	6	5	4	1	16
The job had been more satisfying	1	4	1	2	8
Other	27	16	9	10	62
	46	39	25	21	131

The interesting fact about Table 17 is that few ex-pastors who said lack of enjoyment of the work was an important cause for their leaving, also reported that they would have stayed had the work been more satisfying. This evidence was supported when we cross-tabulated "didn't enjoy work" with 10 questions on the satisfactions found in work. Those who did not find satisfaction in their jobs, were not significantly those who did not enjoy their work.

We then explored two areas of work: the enjoyment of role tasks and satisfaction gained from work.

Enjoyment of Work

Samuel Blizzard (1956) documented how clergymen feel about their various work-connected duties. He interviewed over 500 clergymen to find what they spend their time doing, and what they consider important. The clergymen ranked the various roles expected of them in terms of their own enjoyment, amount of time spent, and the importance of the job. The rankings are shown below. There is very little relationship between what the men considered important and what they spent their time doing.* There is also little relationship between what they enjoyed and what they spent their time doing.†

Attitudes of Clergymen About Their Various Roles			
Role	Importance	Enjoyment	Time Spent
Preacher	1	2	3
Pastor	2	1	2
Priest	3	4	4
Teacher	4	3	6
Organizer	5	6	5
Administrator	6	5	1

Both groups in our study were asked to rate their enjoyment of some of their major activities. They were given a six-point scale from "disliked very much" (1) to "enjoyed very much" (6) on which to rate the activity.

We looked at the same work roles that Blizzard reported for the sake of comparison. Table 18 analyzes the high enjoyment of these roles by both the ex-pastors and the pastors on the basis of their rating the activity either 5 or 6 on the scale.

In terms of which activities were most enjoyed and least enjoyed, the rank order shows little difference between the ex-pastors and the pastors. However, when one looks at the proportion of each group that highly enjoyed an activity, a difference may be observed.

The activities that the pastors enjoyed substantially more than the ex-pastors are those that strictly delineate the parish minister—preaching, helping individuals to Christian commitment, and general calling in homes. Thirteen to 16 percent more pastors enjoyed these activities than did ex-pastors.

The only activity which the ex-pastors enjoyed substantially more than the pastors is that which had no formal church connection—giving leadership to the community on crucial social issues. The greatest similarities in enjoyment are in activities that are found equally in many professions—serious study and counsel-

* A Spearman's rho, a measure of the statistical significance of association in ranked data, was .1 in a scale of -1 to $+1$. Zero indicates no relationship.
† Spearman's rho $= .23$.

Table 18. High Enjoyment of Role Activities

| | NUMBER OF 5 OR 6 RATINGS BY | | | | | |
| | EX–PASTORS | | | PASTORS | | |
	No.	Percent	Rank	No.	Percent	Rank
Preaching	76	58.0	2	183	73.2	1
Counseling (pastor)	95	72.5	1	179	71.6	2
General calling in homes (pastor)	44	33.6	*	116	46.4	*
Helping individuals to Christian commitment (priest)	68	51.9	4	169	67.6	3
Teaching adults and young people (teacher)	71	54.2 ⎫	3	155	62.0 ⎫	4
Serious study (teacher)	71	54.2 ⎭		128	51.6 ⎭	
Judicatory activity (organization)	33	25.2 ⎫	5	70	27.8 ⎫	5
Programming church group activity (organization)	28	21.4 ⎭		75	30.0 ⎭	
Conducting meetings (administration)	25	19.1	6	58	23.2	6
Community leadership on crucial social issues	75	57.3		112	44.8	

* General calling, though a pastoral task theoretically, appears greatly out of order in the ranking. One wonders if the emphasis in many local churches on the pastor's calling on new members in order to attract them, has the effect of taking this duty from the pastoral category and putting it into the organizational category.

ing. Other than preaching, the activities that the ex-pastors enjoyed the most when they were in the church were those which they could do equally well in secular employment.

There is a sharp delineation between preacher-priest-pastor-teacher and organizer-administrator among both pastors and ex-pastors. The former roles are geared toward professional goals; the latter are geared toward organizational goals. Among both pastors and ex-pastors general calling in homes was enjoyed nearly as little as administration-organization.

JOB SATISFACTION

Satisfaction with work implies the meeting of some internal standard set by a person. This standard is composed of his personal values, general social values, and the values set by the profession.

The pastor has been socialized in seminary into holding a definite set of values. He has been trained to do a job on the basis of these values. His peers in seminary and the faculty have reinforced the values, and his own ideal of himself as a clergyman has been formed. This idea of his professional self we shall call his professional self-image. For many kinds of work, but especially in the professions, the professional self-image encompasses the other parts of life until they are practically inseparable. The clergyman's professional self-image is his total definition of himself.

The pastor enters the local church with his own ideas of what his role entails. He knows what he should be and what he should do in the system. The people in the local church, however, do not have his specialized understanding of his role. They usually have different ideas of what they want him to do. If the distance between the pastor's definition and the local church's definition of the job is too great, there is role conflict.

Some role conflict is inevitable in any situation where the members of a system are differentially socialized in the system. The members of a church do not understand the theological background of the pastor's action. They understand that they have certain concrete needs and feel that the pastor should pay attention to them first before he gets involved in other activities.

In the United Church of Christ, there are two sources of role conflict: (1) the difference between the pastor's and his congregation's understanding of his role, (2) the difference between the pastor's and the organizational hierarchy's understanding of his role. The latter will be discussed later in terms of professional support. The larger the difference between the role understandings, the more compromise the pastor has to make with his self-image, and the more dissatisfied he is with the job.

A professional entering a local church makes certain assumptions. He assumes that people are interested in moving toward more fully committed lives and that his work will make a difference. He assumes that his congregation will appreciate his work toward that end. He assumes that the local church situation provides him with an opportunity to move creatively toward his professional goals and that he will be able to use himself fully in this situation.

We measured satisfaction in three ways: (1) internal success or satisfaction with the results of work, (2) external success or satisfaction with members' appreciation of the work, and (3) long-range successes or satisfaction with the use of abilities and congruence of job with self-image. A series of statements was provided to measure satisfaction and dissatisfaction. They were marked on a scale from 1 (very dissatisfied) to 6 (very satisfied). Men who responded with 1 or 2 were considered "dissatisfied" and those who responded with 5 or 6 were considered "satisfied."

Both the ex-pastors and the pastors were dissatisfied with the direct results of their work or with the work of the laymen in the church. Table 19 illustrates this dissatisfaction. They were especially dissatisfied with members' willingness to study and witness in the world.

To be appreciated by the local church members is a sign of outward success to a minister. We asked both the pastors and the ex-pastors, How well satisfied were you with the congregation's appreciation of your work? Five percent more ex-pastors were dissatisfied with the congregation's appreciation and 11 percent fewer were satisfied. The results are presented in Table 20.

Table 19. Satisfaction and Dissatisfaction with Member Activity in Last Church

ACTIVITY SATISFACTION WITH:	EX–PASTORS		PASTORS	
	NUMBER	PERCENT	NUMBER	PERCENT
Willingness to study				
Dissatisfied	45	34.35	81	32.40
Satisfied	17	12.22	32	12.80
Willingness to witness in the world				
Dissatisfied	46	35.11	68	27.20
Satisfied	7	5.34	23	9.20
Shared leadership in church				
Dissatisfied	23	17.00	43	17.20
Satisfied	32	24.43	61	24.40

Table 20. Satisfaction and Dissatisfaction with Aspects of Last Church Position

ASPECT OF THE JOB SATISFACTION WITH:	EX–PASTORS		PASTORS	
	NUMBER	PERCENT	NUMBER	PERCENT
Congregation's appreciation				
Dissatisfied	18	13.74	22	8.80
Satisfied	39	29.77	103	41.20
Possibility of contribution to that organization				
Dissatisfied	35	26.72	21	8.40
Satisfied	23	17.55	105	42.00
Opportunity for creative leadership				
Dissatisfied	29	22.3	34	13.60
Satisfied	37	28.24	100	40.00
Utilization of strengths instead of weaknesses				
Dissatisfied	23	17.56	31	12.40
Satisfied	31	23.55	97	38.80

Three additional questions attempted to discover how well the last church job fulfilled the professional self-image of clergymen. We felt these questions measured the internal success factors. The questions were: 1. How well satisfied were you with the possibility that you could make a significant contribution to the vitality and mission of that organization? (This question measured satisfaction with goal activity.) 2. How well satisfied were you with the opportunity to exert creative leadership and try out new ideas? (This question measured satisfaction with day-to-day tasks.) 3. How well satisfied were you with the degree to which the work utilized your strengths rather than your weaknesses as a minister? (This question got at personal variation in the job.) The results are shown in Table 20.

There is a definite difference in the perception by the pastors and ex-pastors of the opportunities to be of fullest use in their church. The pastors were more satisfied in their jobs than were the ex-pastors. The probability is slight that this difference was due to the actual church situation, since both groups were dissatisfied with their members' actions in the church. The difference is due to an internal expectation of what the job should be.

The ex-pastors were asked the difference between their job satisfaction in the pastorate and in their current job. Fifty-one percent, or 68 of the 131, have more job satisfaction now. Of these, 27 report higher satisfaction due to the importance of the work and their own productivity.

When the pertinent dominant reasons for leaving are cross-tabulated with the pertinent responses to "I would have stayed if," we get a group of ex-pastors who left primarily because of lack of job satisfaction (Table 21). The data show this lack of satisfaction to be a result of different perceptions of what the job should be. With the traditional local church's understanding of the role, the ex-pastor feels he is unable to meet the major goals of effecting change. One man put it this way, "I felt that much of my work was trivial in comparison to the layman's work. Rather, it was the laymen who were in the position to make the decisions and to do the acting. I feel it is the laity who are holding the church back."

The dissatisfaction with the work of the church points to a breakdown of the system. First, there seems to be lack of congruence between the manpower needs of the system and the training of professionals. The pastor entering the local church has his own goals for that church, set during his training and socialization period. The church also has its goals both implicit and explicit which need fulfilling. The pastor is often unable to be fulfilled while pursuing the goals of the local church. Second, the needs of the local church should be explicit in order to hire pastors who find their professional fulfillment while doing the kind of work needed by a specific church.

REWARDS

While satisfaction with a job is an implicit reward, generally speaking, rewards refer to monetary and fringe benefits or explicit rewards. There is little doubt that the ministry is the poorest paying profession. Starting salaries of pastors are even less than starting salaries of teachers in most states.

In comparing the ex-pastors with the pastors, we see a significant difference

Table 21. Job Satisfaction Reasons for Leaving and
Would Have Stayed If Job More Satisfying

	DOMINANT REASONS FOR LEAVING		
WOULD HAVE STAYED IF:	COULDN'T GET CHURCH TO GROW, OR NOT CHALLENGED	OPPORTUNITY TO PUT TRAINING TO FULL USE	TOTAL
Church was interested in a new kind of ministry	6	2	8
The role of the minister was defined differently	0	2	2
The church or job was more satisfying	1	1	2
	7	5	12

Table 22. Satisfaction with Salary and Living Conditions

	EX–PASTORS		PASTORS	
	NUMBER	PERCENT	NUMBER	PERCENT
Dissatisfied	23	17.55	16	6.40
Satisfied	30	22.90	123	49.20

between their responses. Table 22 presents this difference. Eleven percent more ex-pastors than pastors were dissatisfied with salary and living conditions. Twenty-six percent more pastors than ex-pastors were satisfied with salary and living conditions.

Why does a pastor who has had three years or more of professional training in addition to a regular four-year college course agree to the low salary offered to him?

First, one of the primary values of Christianity is that of selfless service to people regardless of their ability to pay. The young pastor feels it selfish to haggle for a higher salary from people who cannot afford to pay him any more. A second reason for low salaries is the economic fact of supply and demand. There are still enough ministers to fill the churches' needs, even many of the small, poor churches which continue in existence.

The question remains, Do pastors leave because of poor salaries? The answer is Yes and No. There are very few who leave the church solely because they do not make enough money. Table 23 shows the pertinent answers to the dominant reasons for leaving and "would have stayed if" questions.

Only five of the ex-pastors left the church primarily because of lack of money. Lest the church feel smug, however, 12.69 percent, or 14, rated inadequate sal-

Table 23. Dominant Reasons for Leaving

Would Have Stayed If:	Money	Other	Total
I had more money or better living conditions	5	5	10
Other	5	0	5
	10	5	15

ary and living conditions a highly important reason for leaving; and many others were dissatisfied with their salary and living conditions. So while few pastors leave because of low salary, it is a condition in many other reasons for leaving. In order to ascertain some of the possible ways that low salary contributes to other reasons, we must see what money means in our culture.

Money is an important reward for several reasons. First, it enables a man to live comfortably and enjoy some of the luxuries of life. Second, it makes him feel that he is fulfilling his function as a husband and father by providing for his family. Finally, it is a measure of his success in the community and even to the members of his parish who tend to judge success by secular standards.

A salary is a relative reward. It depends not only on the cost of living, but also on the alternative jobs available and what they pay. Thus if a pastor makes more than parishioners, he may feel satisfied with his salary even though it is smaller than that of a colleague who makes more but whose parishioners' salaries are higher.

While, as we saw, few clergymen are leaving the church expressly because of low salaries, the lack of money indirectly influences their leaving in three ways:

1. Many pastors moonlight in order to make more money. This gives them a foot in another job system which they may then move into. The other job system may be comparatively more satisfying in a professional way so that the decision to leave is facilitated. Twenty-one ex-pastors, or 16 percent, found employment because of their activity, either a part-time job or voluntary work, in another system. This process will become clearer in the next chapter.

2. The pastor's wife may have to work to bring in money. This may make the pastor feel more inadequate as a husband and man, also less satisfied; and eventually he may look for another job.

3. Finally, his own values as he is more removed from seminary and peer influence are more amenable to the values of the culture. One of these values is that if a man is a success, he will make enough money. If he is a success, when he changes jobs the new job will pay considerably more. Consequently, he may think of himself as unsuccessful and defeated. While he may or may not leave the ministry, he will be a less effective pastor.

OTHER REWARDS

Many of the people who hire clergymen are quick to counter accusations of low wages with glowing reports of fringe benefits such as free housing, car allowances, retirement and social security benefits. Let us give some of these items a quick once-over.

First of all, what about the free housing? There are several reasons why providing benefits such as housing instead of comparable cash is undesirable: 1. The person is denied the free choice. A pastor, as any other person taking a job, should have the freedom to have the kind of housing he chooses. 2. The housing is often very near the church. This puts a strain on the pastor on his day off and on his family most of the time. 3. If the pastor were allowed the freedom to house himself, he could choose to buy his housing, which would build equity for his retirement years.

In addition to this, the laymen often put an exorbitant value on the free housing, equating it with their own. In a study of 5,623 Protestant clergymen by the National Council of Churches, the median value of housing in 1963 was $1,300 (Scherer, 1964, p. 3). The housing is not necessarily of the same quality as the layman's. Moreover, as homeowners, laymen build some equity in the house. Their taxes and mortgages also provide income tax breaks.

Second, what about the car allowance? In the same study reported above, clergymen reported a mean *loss* of $685 per year on automobile expenses (*ibid.,* p. 8).

What about retirement benefits? The individual church decides what percentage (up to 11 percent) of the pastor's salary it will pay. In the NCC's study, a median of $589 was paid by the churches to 74 percent of the clergymen (*ibid.,* p. 7). Even though this amount is considered part of his salary, in many associations, should the pastor decide to go into secular work, he loses that part of the retirement paid by the local church.

What about social security? It took the U.S. government to insist that clergymen must have social security benefits. Clergymen are considered self-employed even though they are not. How many local churches raised the salary of their pastors to meet the cost of those social security payments?

Even with benefits added, the NCC study shows that the median clergy salary is less than the median salary for teachers, factory foremen, sales personnel, and salaried managers and officials (*ibid.,* p. 5).

WORKING CONDITIONS

The ex-pastors reported appallingly bad working conditions. They have cold, unattractive offices, ill-furnished, with little regular secretarial help. They have one day off a week at the most. They have irregular working hours and are often called on in emergency situations without compensatory time off. Even if they are the senior professionals in the organization, they often do not have supervisory powers over other personnel such as choir directors and religious education personnel. Their wives are often expected to serve without salary and are often criticized for their participation or lack of it. Twenty-six ex-pastors, or 19 percent, mentioned improved working conditions as their first spontaneous response to the question of difference in life in secular work.

The most oppressive of the working conditions is the overwork. Though a pastor is often up night after night at meetings, his parishioners expect him to be available in the early mornings as well. He seldom has a weekend free to be with his family doing the things that other families do on weekends. We asked the question, How satisfied were you with the amount of time you had for family and private life? The responses from both the ex-pastors and pastors are in Table 24. The ex-pastors were both less dissatisfied and less satisfied with the time

Table 24. Satisfaction with Time for Family and Private Life

| | EX–PASTORS | | PASTORS | |
	NUMBER	PERCENT	NUMBER	PERCENT
Dissatisfied	32	24.32	69	27.60
Satisfied	23	17.56	74	29.60

they had for family and private life. The poor working conditions, like the low rewards, seldom are a direct cause for a pastor leaving the church; however, their influence on other causes such as family troubles, physical breakdown, and the readiness to accept an unsolicited job should not be minimized. The UCC, at the national level, instead of insisting on humane standards, continues to send out material to ministers fostering the nineteenth-century picture of the pastor, chiding him for not being at his office every day, dressed appropriately, and reinforcing an image that cannot but produce guilt in the dedicated but human being who is in the parish.

SUPPORT SYSTEMS

Few professionals have the same conception of their roles as do their clients or their administrative bosses. Doctors notoriously conflict both with hospital administrators and with patients. Social workers, lawyers, schoolteachers, all conceive of their roles in specialized terms which may be in conflict with the more practical concerns of administrators or the more self-centered concerns of the client.

A clergyman has a role-set composed of laymen in his congregation, colleagues, his board, the leaders of the various judicatories, the leaders of other churches in the community, council of churches, etc. Each of the people who interacts with him has an expectation of what his role should be. All the expectations in addition to his own understanding of what his job is, are likely to cause conflict and tension within the pastor as to his role. Robert Merton believes that this is basically a structural problem in an occupational system and that society provides various mechanisms which tend to reduce the conflict and tension (Merton, 1957, pp. 106 ff.).

Some mechanisms that minimize tension and conflict work very poorly in the system of the church. One of these is mutual support among status occupants. By this Merton means that actual or possible tension and conflict between a clergyman and his laymen or judicatory officials or board of trustees is not likely to be an isolated occurrence but is common to all occupants of similar positions. Unions and professional societies are a means of mutual support to counteract the power of the role-set to define the role. Not only do they provide social support, but they develop mutually accepted standards which anticipate and therefore soften future conflict.

This author interviewed 40 ex-pastors of several denominations in preparation for this study. Thirty-two of them opened the interview with a remark about the uniqueness of their particular situation. In fact, the same story was told time after time. Clergymen, who are supposed to love everyone, be patient to a fault, wise, just, and competent in all areas, seem to feel it an expression of inadequacy to confess less than perfect relationships with their laymen or denominational executives.

Professional Peer Support

Clergymen form organizations of two kinds. The first kind is denominational bodies. The local association and the state conference are composed of all the UCC pastors as well as the association and conference staff. Lay delegates from each local church are also members of these bodies. When a pastor wants to change jobs, he must depend upon the staff of the association and conference to recommend him. He is not likely, therefore, to bring up either professional or personal problems for discussion in these organizations. These bodies are not particularly supporting to the pastor in his conflict with his role-set, because they comprise part of his problem.

Both the ex-pastors and the pastors expressed the same feelings toward other UCC pastors. We asked three questions: 1. How much would you have valued the praise of other UCC pastors? 2. How supportive were fellow pastors of your denomination? 3. How isolating were fellow pastors of your denomination? The answers were on a six-point scale from "not at all" (1) to "extremely much" (6). Table 25 shows the responses from both ex-pastors and pastors. Low includes ratings 1 and 2, and high includes ratings 5 and 6.

The second kind of organizations that clergymen form are ecumenical or across denominational lines. Some of these formal organizations sponsored by a council of churches. They are usually organized around some particular task such as teacher training, or racial justice activities, or fair housing, etc. Others are informal community groups which meet together to discuss common problems. The latter sound as though they are supportive organizations. However, on examining the agenda of most of these ministeriums—even the name sounds ecclesiastical—they have speakers and discussions on commonly recognized concerns but not the secret, worrisome problems which might indicate inadequacy in the profession.

The same three questions were asked about feelings toward other pastors in the community. The same kinds of response were found. Table 26 presents the results.

Professional peers both of the same denomination and of the community have little influence on the feelings of isolation that the minister has. While neither the

Table 25. Feelings of Pastors and Ex-Pastors
Toward Their Fellow UCC Peers

	EX–PASTORS		PASTORS	
How Much Did You:	Number	Percent	Number	Percent
Value praise				
Low	22	16.79	35	14.00
High	40	30.53	67	26.80
Feel support from				
Low	44	33.68	64	25.60
High	32	24.43	50	20.00
Feel isolated by				
Low	67	51.14	126	50.40
High	20	15.27	29	11.60

Table 26. Feelings of Pastors and Ex-Pastors Toward
Other Pastors in the Community

	EX–PASTORS		PASTORS	
How Much Did You:	Number	Percent	Number	Percent
Value praise				
Low	27	20.61	30	16.00
High	36	27.53	64	25.60
Feel support from				
Low	43	32.83	65	26.00
High	26	19.85	48	19.20
Feel isolated by				
Low	66	50.38	112	44.80
High	16	12.21	33	9.20

pastor nor the ex-pastor has felt isolated *by* his professional peers, he does feel isolated *from* them. We discovered this by asking each man if he had close friends in each of these groups. The responses were: none, one or two, and several. We asked ex-pastors if they had sought the advice of these friends about leaving church employment. The pastors were asked if they would seek such advice. Table 27 shows that the ex-pastors were more isolated from their peers than the

Table 27. Friends of and Advice from Professional Peers

	EX–PASTORS		PASTORS	
	NUMBER	PERCENT	NUMBER	PERCENT
Friends among other UCC pastors				
None	19	14.50	19	7.60
One or two	49	37.40	83	33.20
Several	56	42.75	138	55.20
	124	94.65	240	96.00
Friends among other pastors				
None	35	26.72	42	16.40
One or two	43	32.82	114	45.60
Several	48	36.64	83	33.20
	126	96.18	238	95.20
Seek advice of UCC pastors				
Yes	57	43.51	194	77.60
No	54	41.22	34	13.60
	111	84.73	228	91.20
Seek advice of other pastors				
Yes	32	24.43	144	57.60
No	75	57.25	76	30.40
	107	81.68	220	88.00

pastors. Thirteen percent more pastors than ex-pastors had several friends among UCC ministers. Pastors tend to seek advice about career change more than ex-pastors.

DENOMINATIONAL EXECUTIVES

We come now to a very special case of professional peers, the denominational executives. The denominational executive has little formal power over the pastor in the UCC. However, his good opinion is necessary in that all-important job change. He can recommend—or fail to recommend—a pastor for a new position, or he can give him a lukewarm reference which will greatly damage his career. Therefore, as is expected, the pastors and ex-pastors valued the praise of the denominational executive much more than that of their other professional peers. Table 28 shows the difference between pastors and ex-pastors toward denominational executives and other ministers in the UCC.

We looked at the 67 ex-pastors who valued the praise of the denominational executives to see if they had received their support. When we cross-tabulated this

Table 28. Feelings Toward Denominational Executives and Other UCC Peers

How Much Did You:	FEELINGS TOWARD DENOMINATIONAL EXECUTIVES				FEELINGS TOWARD OTHER UCC PEERS			
	Ex-Pastors		Pastors		Ex-Pastors		Pastors	
	Number	Percent	Number	Percent	Number	Percent	Number	Percent
Value praise								
Low	18	13.74	26	10.40	22	16.79	35	14.00
High	67	51.15	106	42.40	40	30.53	67	26.80
Feel support from								
Low	49	37.40	44	17.60	44	33.68	64	25.60
High	45	34.35	76	30.40	32	24.43	50	20.00
Feel isolated by								
Low	67	51.14	147	58.80	67	51.14	126	50.40
High	27	20.61	18	7.20	20	15.27	29	11.60

variable with several others, we found that, of this 67, 20 felt not at all supported by the denominational executive, 14 felt extremely isolated by him, and 6 felt an important reason for having left the church was coercion by the denominational leadership.

We mentioned previously that the organizational expectation of the pastor's role may be a source of role conflict for the pastor. The church executive must be concerned in part with keeping appropriations up, keeping people in the parish happy, doing the committee work of the conference. His contact with the local pastor is through these organizational activities. It is only natural for him to reward with excellent personal recommendations the pastor who has successfully filled organizational functions.

Therefore, the pastor who has been more "Christian" or made the most impact in his laymen's lives or on the community is not necessarily the one who is rewarded by the system. It makes little organizational sense to put a "troublemaker" in a wealthy church. Such a person might alienate parishioners, causing them to withdraw their support. The role expected and rewarded by the denominational executive is thus sometimes contrary to the role definition of the professional. It appears to him that in order to be successful in his career in the church, he must do the job the organizational way and not the professional way. The conflict causes great dissatisfaction within the professional and therefore causes him to look for alternatives where he can be more effective—once again the dual goals, though very necessary, are in conflict with each other.

There is a discrepancy between the organizational function of the denominational executive and his pastoral function. If he serves as a strictly administrative person, he need not be a pastor. If he serves as a supportive person, then he should be divorced from the reward functions. Conflict between organizational-administrative goals and professional goals is inevitable. Perhaps the same person cannot adequately fill both functions.

We could say that many ministers are indeed isolated from their professional peers. It is true that some of this isolation may be due to the kind of people who choose to enter the ministry. It is definitely true, however, that part of it is due to a gap in the support system, the support system which most occupations and professions have. Clergymen feel cohesion with neither the pastors of their own denomination nor with the profession as a whole. They have no strong central body which sets standards, gives them comfort, and protects them against unfair labor practices. They have what is commonly called in other organizations a company union. In this union, they are unable to bring up real grievances because the leader of the union is also an owner of the company.

LAY SUPPORT

We mentioned earlier that society provides some mechanisms which serve to reduce the conflict that inevitably arises between any worker and others in his role-set who help to define his role. Professional support which we have just analyzed was one of them. A second mechanism is the natural insulation of role activity from observability. A person in a professional position seldom interacts with all the members of his role-set continuously. He is able to work without tension even though he may be at odds with some people. However, few professionals are as visible in all their actions as are clergymen. A physician can make a decision on the health of a patient which other patients might not agree to, but they have no knowledge of it. If a clergyman works for fair housing or works long hours on his sermons instead of calling on his parishioners, nearly everyone in his role-set is apt to be aware of it. Not only is the clergyman visible to his role-set, but he interacts with them frequently. Therefore, if conflict exists about his actions, the clergyman finds it difficult to escape.

Pastors valued the praise of their lay leaders more than ex-pastors did. They also felt more supported by their lay leaders and less isolated by them. If we check the results in Table 29 against the feelings of pastors and ex-pastors to-

Table 29. Feelings of Pastors and Ex-Pastors Toward Their Lay Leaders

How Much Did You:	EX–PASTORS		PASTORS	
	Number	Percent	Number	Percent
Value praise				
Low	5	3.81	2	.80
High	72	54.96	151	60.40
Feel support from				
Low	16	12.21	15	6.00
High	53	40.46	130	52.00
Feel isolated by				
Low	57	43.51	42	50.40
High	19	14.50	18	7.20

ward both other UCC ministers and denominational executives (Table 28), we find some interesting comparisons.

1. 33.6 percent more pastors valued the praise of lay leaders than the praise of other UCC ministers, as compared with 24.43 percent more ex-pastors.

2. 18 percent more pastors valued the praise of lay leaders than the praise of denominational executives as compared with only 3.81 percent difference for the ex-pastors.

3. 32 percent more pastors felt much support from the lay leaders than felt much support from other UCC ministers, as compared with 16.03 of the ex-pastors.

4. 21.6 percent more pastors felt much support from the lay leaders than felt much support from denominational executives as compared with 6.11 percent of the ex-pastors.

The lay leaders are a more important part of the minister's role-set than his professional peers or the denominational executive. He values their praise, and he needs their support and gets it. However, in any situation where controversial issues are apt to arise, people will disagree. No matter what he does or says, the clergyman will alienate some of his parishioners. One ex-pastor in the study put it this way when asked if he had had any surprises in his first parish.

> Yes, . . . how difficult it was to deal with the congregation with so many different and conflicting feelings. I was frightened by the tension and problems I caused by taking one side or another in certain issues. I couldn't ever please them all. It was a losing battle. No one taught or warned me about these hostilities I would face.

When we look at the importance the ex-pastors gave to conflict with laymen as a cause for leaving, along with several other variables, we can see how conflict affects other areas. Thirty percent, or 6 ex-pastors who considered such conflict a cause of leaving, left because of personal or professional inadequacies as the dominant reason. Fifty-five percent, or 12 ex-pastors who considered conflict with laymen a cause, felt some urgency to leave because of pressure from laymen. However, 3 of 20 ex-pastors who considered conflict with laymen a cause for leaving, still felt support from laymen. This does not mean that the data are unreliable. A clergyman may feel supported by 95 percent of his laymen and still feel forced to leave by the efforts of the remaining 5 percent. This is the way the system is structured.

The system also fails to provide clergymen with tools to deal with the inevitable conflict and tension. Twenty-three ex-pastors who considered conflict with laymen a cause for leaving, also said that they were ill prepared by the seminary to deal with the practicalities of a parish. Lack of training puts an unnecessary handicap on the professional in a system already far from perfect.

THE FAMILY

The more areas of life that an occupation invades, the harder it is to get rid of frustrations and anxieties which build up during the normal work day. A clergyman works many more than 40 hours a week. Often his days off are not as sacred as they should be. Sometimes his social life is with parishioners. Even many of his neighbors belong to his church. So a clergyman's free time is not really as free as it seems. This situation puts a great strain on the family.

When we asked the open-ended question, What difference has it made in your marriage and family life to be out of the pastoral ministry? the answers were surprisingly congruent (Table B28). The cross-tabulation with the item describing husband-wife relationships at the time of the decision to leave showed that even ex-pastors whose marital relationships were good found their family situations happier or greatly improved. The change of occupation itself, not the individual family situation, is the cause of this improvement.

This topic is explored in detail in chapter 5. The data lead us to say that there are strains upon the family of a clergyman in the occupational system of the church. We can cite several reasons. First, the value system of the church has long included as the image of the good pastor, one who forsakes father, mother, sister, and brother to do God's will. It is a picture of a long-suffering servant. The UCC as well as other denominations is still sending out material from central offices which supports this image.

Second, the job definition of the pastor is vague and general. Even in a small church, there is rarely enough time for the pastor to do everything he feels should be done. This leads him to overwork and takes him away from his family.

Third, society's picture of the most masculine man is aggressive and dominant. Such a picture is contrary to the goody-goody expectations that most local churches have of their pastor. This nonmasculine expectation can cause conflict in a personal relationship where masculinity is extremely desirable. One of the ex-pastors said, "People treated me as though I was neither male nor female. I was some sort of eunuch."

Problems of Interpersonal Relations

We asked the ex-pastors about the difference in their relationships with other people since they left the pastorate. This was an open-ended question and we expected many different kinds of answers. The responses, however, were unexpectedly congruent. Forty-one ex-pastors said that their relationships were better. They were no longer defined by their role as a pastor but as a human being.

Eleven ex-pastors said that their relationships with others are more constructive and realistic. Ten said that their relationships are more satisfying, closer, and more creative. Five now have broader relationships with more people and different kinds of people than in the pastorate. A total of 67 of the 116 ex-pastors who answered this question, or 58 percent, have improved relationships in nonpastoral situations.

In an effort to deal with personality problems and/or improve relationships with their parishioners, some ministers turn to a form of therapy such as group therapy or psychoanalysis, or to a sensitivity training program. A total of 28 ex-pastors had had some such experience either in the past or currently. Another 25 had some personality problems. When we cross-tabulated the question about change of relationships in secular work with personality problems we found that approximately half of both groups reported improved relationships.

The occupational system of the church puts a certain strain on the personality system, especially in having to deal with the inevitable conflict in defining one's own role. We do not have comparable data on the pastors. However, from the vehement responses that the pastors made to some of the questions (see chapter 1), we feel safe in assuming that they are under the same strains.

Conclusion

We reiterate that the organization of the church has some structural elements which prevent it from adequately meeting the employment needs of its professionals. These elements are present regardless of whether the professional meets the need of the system, regardless of whether he has lost his faith, regardless of whether he is competent.

We have shown the strains to be present in the training system, the hiring system, the work and reward system, the support systems, and the family and personality systems. We have shown that most of the strains are currently being experienced by many of the pastors as they have been by the ex-pastors. The strains are handled differently by different people.

An individual clergyman comes to a decision either consciously or subconsciously that the system is not meeting enough of his needs to balance what he has to contribute to it. What does he do? Alvin Gouldner (1960, p. 269) says that he has three alternatives: 1. He can try to change the system so that more of his needs are being met. 2. He can remain in the system for his formal work but participate in other systems in order to meet some of his needs. 3. He can leave the system because the alternatives seem better able to meet his needs.

Some pastors employed in the church find their occupational needs completely met by the church. Many pastors employed in the church are not satisfied by the system. Of the latter, some will work on the denominational board, local and national councils of churches, fund raising committees, church school curriculum, in new ministries, etc., in order to change the system so that more of their needs are met. Some will serve a church and work part time in another system, or lead social revolutions, or serve on YMCA boards, or run for an elective office to meet occupational needs that are inadequately met by the system. Some will leave . . .

5 / OCCUPATIONAL COMMITMENT
AND CAREER DECISIONS

The professional ministry is a high-commitment occupation. Those who enter it are highly committed, and those who continue in it must sustain a similarly strong dedication. Decisions to leave it mark either the withdrawal of that commitment or its radical transformation. The task of this chapter is to analyze these decisions.

Among ex-pastors, only 1 man in 7 would describe himself as having "left the ministry." On the contrary, many took pains to identify their present employment as ministry. The decision to enter secular work is thus for most men not simply a rejection of ministry but a *redefinition* of it to fit nonchurch employment. Virtually none began with such a definition; but most now hold it firmly, continuing their ministries in jobs which range from baker to airline executive and from probation officer to foundation director. Although the decisions were often painful and few left without regret, nearly half report feeling freer, more adequate, or generally better about themselves since making the break, while only a handful feel worse (Table B27).

The place to begin a discussion of career decision-making is with the self-concept as the focus of integration within a person. Theorists of career development have described the process by which a young man or woman develops and tests his own understanding of himself and gradually implements it in the choice of career (Super, 1957). In mid-career the relationship of self-concept and career decision is somewhat different but no less crucial. The image of one's occupational location ("I am a minister") is buttressed by other dimensions: "I *like* being a minister." "I am an *effective* minister." *"Others respond* to my ministry; it is what I *ought* to be doing."

Each person is involved in a web of relationships or interacting systems, and the imperatives of these systems support or undermine the self-concept which serves as the basis of his occupational commitment. The evidence of this study suggests that ministers enter secular employment not because they do not want

to be ministers but rather because of a growing inconsistency between the imperatives of faith, family, church, and society. As changes occur at these various levels,
steady pressures of many kinds create intense strains which the minister is unable to reduce and which create in him a growing frustration. The decision to
move out of church employment most often results from a losing struggle to maintain integrity of performance in a fragmenting job.

To return from sociological to psychological images, a man's commitment to
the professional ministry is strengthened as his self-concept is validated by his
experience of success, pleasure, and appropriateness in his work. His occupational commitment is undermined when his experiences *fail* to confirm his self-
concept and instead raise doubts about the appropriateness of his being in the
ministry. Many such doubts can be and are dispelled, and the minister—like others—finds himself working to reduce the inner dissonance between beliefs about
self and the feedback of experience. However, as a core of unresolved dissatisfaction grows (a growth which may be very rapid but often is the result of years
of experience), his commitment to church ministry is seriously undermined. He
takes more seriously the possibility of other kinds of work because his optimism
about changing the frustrating aspects of his present ministry is fading. At this
point, where hope and frustration are rather delicately balanced, the minister is
open to many possibilities, any of which may serve as a "tipping point" to move
him in the direction of secular employment. The critical factor in such a move,
our theory suggests, is whether he can maintain continuity of self-concept (by re-
defining ministry, by developing a new understanding of self, or—more likely—
both) that will be satisfactorily implemented and supported in a new occupation.

The thesis that runs throughout this book is that the combined impact of
changes in church, society, family, and faith systems has produced in many ministers a delicate balance of hope and frustration which makes them vulnerable to
tipping point experiences, and that out of this situation many have moved to a
redefinition of self or of ministry which leads to career-change decisions. It is our
further conviction that this situation is widespread in the ministry today and that
ex-pastors are in many cases not the castoffs of a stable system, but the bellweth-
ers of massive changes yet to come. We will examine the effects of church, society, family, and faith in the next four sections, then take up the redefinition of
self-concept and vocation, and conclude with a discussion of the decision-making
process.

The Changing Church

Chapter 4 has described the church as an occupational system in which the
needs of its professional leadership are being frustrated by sluggish mobility
channels, inadequate salary and living conditions, a low level of response to the
minister's leadership efforts, and a "support system" which often seems to isolate
rather than to support the pastor in his work. Other writers have suggested that
these conditions exist throughout American Christendom. Hadden (1969) describes the growing polarization between the laity and the clergy, especially the

"new breed," on crucial issues of church life. Role expectations of the minister, the definitions of authority and responsibility, the concept of the church purpose and meaning, and even basic issues of belief demonstrate the widening gap. The resulting strains gradually create an identity crisis for the clergyman as his leadership is repeatedly frustrated and the traditional support systems fail to function.

Among Roman Catholics there are comparable problems as the church modernizes. Fichter (1968) describes the post-Vatican II polarization between younger and older priests and between bishops and parish clergy over crucial questions of church life. As the church changes, the strains are most keenly felt by its parish ministers. Kennedy (1968) points out how "the sensitive, perceptive, and committed clergyman" will suffer more than the marginally adjusted person in the breakdown of older models and the painful emergence of new ways. Under such conditions increasing dissatisfaction raises career questions for the minister, and the organizational imperatives tend to undermine rather than strengthen his career commitment.

The Impact of Social Change

Although our study was not directed to the measurement of change in American life, the interviews revealed the impact of social change clearly in the form of frequent references to frustration growing out of the irrelevance of church life to a changing society. For example, nearly two thirds of the ex-pastors reported disillusionment "with the church's relevance to problems of the modern world" as an important reason for leaving. In describing influences of their theological views in recent years, at least a third cited "value changes in our culture," "rapid scientific and technological development," and "urbanization and secularization in society."

The very rate of contemporary change has destroyed the assumption that a career is a unitary and stable experience of an individual through his life-span. The events of the past 20 years have increased both the mobility of workers and the rate at which their acquired skills become obsolete. Men and women who formerly would have pursued the same occupation until retirement, and for whom occupation and family would have been the twin focuses of stability, are now faced with a radical change in their work life and the need to adapt in very fundamental ways.

These dynamics are part of the secular occupational context in which the clergyman does his ministry. At the same time, the place of philosophical and theological thinking is under attack, the ancient conflict between youth and established power is intensified, the ecology of the city moves more and more of the decision-makers into a white noose around it, or into tall islands within it, and clergymen find that their bread is buttered on the organizational, maintenance side rather than on the prophetic, change-oriented side. When the middle-class person's life is divided spatially between his work and his residence, the church is inevitably identified with his residence, and the minister discovers that he has effectively been peripheralized and the church has been individualized. The decisions are not made in the suburbs, nor are the most pressing problems of the society solved there.

Rapid social change intensifies what has long been a problem for the church; namely, that recruitment and training for the ministry have little relationship to the practice of ministry in the congregational setting. Young people choose the ministry with one set of ideals and occupational images, they are introduced to a radically different set in the seminaries, and when they emerge as neophyte ministers into local parishes they discover additional roles and obligations for which they were never trained. It is a well-nigh universal complaint among younger clergy that they had to learn to be ministers after they left the seminary.

Social change affects the career decisions of the minister in yet another way. While the church as an employment system is no longer expanding and may even be contracting in its personnel needs, the national economy continues to expand, creating many new positions. The impact of managerial and communications revolutions, the struggle against poverty, the explosive growth of educational institutions, and the acceleration of technological change have opened many new doors for men and women with organizational and leadership skills. It is no accident that the largest numbers of clergy moving into secular employment enter social service and education occupations, since these are areas of rapid growth throughout the society. The tighter the job squeeze in the church and the more sluggish its mobility system, the greater will be the lure of new occupations outside. Among many Protestants, vocation is largely regarded as mission, helping, doing good; and many of these secular positions enable such a mission to survive even when stripped of its ecclesiastical context.

The effects of all this upon the career of the minister are enormous. As change becomes the order of the day, as mobility opportunities open and new fields seek out his skills, the minister often perceives himself locked into an institution which he was not trained to manage and whose character he misjudged from the beginning. The erosion of the minister's occupational commitment becomes extremely difficult to resist.

The Family System

Ministers are family men, to whom the attitudes of their wives and the welfare of their children are of great importance. Both ex-pastors and pastors depend upon their immediate families for confirmation of their own values. The family is thus one of the minister's chief *reference groups,* as described by Sherif and Wilson (1953):

> Reference groups might just as well be called *anchoring* groups. The individual's directive attitudes, . . . which define and regulate his behavior to other persons, other groups, and to an important extent even to himself, are formed in relation to the values and norms of his reference groups. They constitute an important basis of his self-identity, of his sense of belongingness, of the core of his social ties.

Groups or persons whose values a minister shares and prizes thus strongly influence his decisions and help to anchor him in the social structure.

To identify the most significant reference groups, we asked for a response to the following item:

> Most of us appreciate receiving praise for work well done. During your pastorate, please indicate how much you would have valued the praise of each of the persons or groups listed below.
> 1. Fellow pastors of same denomination
> 2. Denominational executives who knew your work best
> 3. Lay leaders in congregation
> 4. Wife or husband
> 5. Fellow pastors in churches of same community
> 6. Others on your church staff (if any)
> 7. Close friends not included above

A rating scale from 1 to 6 was given for each of these persons or groups, with the lower end of the valuing scale labeled "not at all" and the higher end "extremely much." We theorized that ratings of 5 or 6 would be given to the groups or persons on whom the minister depends most for affirmation of his values and appreciation of his work. These we would regard as his chief reference groups.

As Table B25 shows, more than three fourths of those responding to this item desired their wives' praise extremely much. The order of decreasing values for each group is as follows:

EX-PASTORS	PASTORS
Wife	Wife
Close friends	Lay leaders
Lay leaders	Close friends
Denominational executive	Others on church staff
Others on church staff	Denominational executive
Fellow UCC pastors	Fellow UCC pastors
Other pastors in community	Other pastors in community

The near unanimity of pastors and ex-pastors in reference orientations is striking. There can be little doubt that the great majority of respondents look to their wives more than to anyone else to confirm the value of their work. (Equally striking is the location of fellow clergy at the bottom of both lists. The significance of this has been discussed in chapter 4.)

This fact appears in another way when we look at the way pastors and ex-pastors responded to the following item.

> Now you are asked to make a slightly different evaluation about these persons or groups: how supportive (helpful) they actually were and how much they tended to isolate or nullify your efforts as pastor.

The same list of persons and groups was given with two additional six-point rating scales, one labeled "highly supportive" and the other "highly isolating." Each scale ran from "not at all" to "extremely much." As discussed in chapter 4, we obtained from this item a measure of the intensity of the minister's *support system,* and we learned which individuals received low support from highly valued reference persons.

Both groups agree that their wives are the most *supportive* of reference persons (Table B26) with 75.8 percent of the ex-pastors and 85.2 percent of the pastors rating her as very supportive. Also, wife shares with close friends the smallest number of "highly isolating" ratings. *The fact that the family is a crucial support structure for the UCC minister as well as his most important reference group makes it obvious that ministers' career decisions are heavily influenced by family relationships.*

The interaction of family and occupational systems represent both an important strength and a glaring weakness of the ministry. As a strength, it provides great resources for men doing a difficult and often lonely job. Our conference and interview experiences reveal how deeply ministers have drawn on this well of strength. At the same time, we are troubled by the lack of professional solidarity exemplified in the low reference and support values given to fellow UCC and other community ministers, who fall at the bottom of Tables B25 and B26. Much strength which could be gained from peers is found instead in the family.

The overdependence on the family, which is suggested by the reference and support data, may be reinforced by the church subculture that tends to make a minister's family life an important professional criterion to be evaluated when he is being considered for employment and when his work is being reviewed. The church also holds many expectations for the minister's wife as part of the ministry, and her deep involvement in her husband's work naturally leads him to give her views and her support high value. The fact that the minister occupies a "total exemplary status" (Mills, 1969) in which neither he nor his family can effectively move beyond their clergy-defined roles at any time, further drives them into mutual dependence and hinders the pastor's development of other reference and support systems.

The experience of ex-pastors demonstrates the significance of family influence on career decisions. In assigning to each of the ex-pastors a dominant reason for his move out, we found that there were no less than 25—out of 131 interviewed —whose moves were primarily the result of family problems, including 10 unhappy wives, 8 divorces or separations, 4 wives with emotional problems, and 3 problems with children. Moreover, in describing changes in their lives resulting from entering secular work, 35.1 percent reported that family problems were a contributing factor in the decision to leave. They were particularly influential in the decisions of men in their 30's and 40's and also among those who have left church employment within the past four years.

While few of these moves can be attributed *solely* to family problems, the fact that the family problems are so prominently recorded in the interviews is strong evidence of the impact of family life upon career decisions. The minister attributes this impact to three important factors: (1) the welfare of his family, (2) his wife's role dissatisfaction, and (3) the coercive power of a marital crisis. The evidence suggests that family welfare is the least prominent of the three patterns in career-change decisions, that wife's role dissatisfaction is the most common, and that marital crisis is the most compelling influence. Of course, a minister's decision may include two or even three of these situations, but dynamically they are different.

FAMILY WELFARE

Several ministers found that concern for the needs of their families was the overriding consideration in moving into secular employment. One minister's wife developed serious emotional problems which were aggravated by the parish situation, while another's children began "acting out" their resentment of his ministry.

In all, nearly half (47.3%) the ex-pastors gave some importance to "family would greatly benefit by move" as a reason for their career decisions, and 38 of these (29%) gave it high importance (Table B22). In assigning dominant reasons for the change, we found that three moves were dictated chiefly by problems with children and four by wives' emotional problems.

THE IMPORTANCE OF WIFE'S ROLE DISSATISFACTION

Because she is his chief reference and support person, the minister's wife's attitudes toward her role are very important to him. Even though dissatisfied, she may support him strongly: 72 percent of the wives who preferred to leave the ministry were nevertheless perceived by their husbands as highly supportive (Table 30). But the discontent of the pastor's wife will undercut her support and reinforce his own dissatisfaction.

Table 30. Ex-Pastors' Wives' Attitudes Toward Leaving, by How Supportive Wife Was

WIFE'S ATTITUDE TOWARD LEAVING	HOW SUPPORTIVE WIFE WAS					
	HIGH	PERCENT	MEDIUM	PERCENT	LOW	PERCENT
Prefers to leave	49	72.0	16	23.5	3	4.4
Neutral	17	81.0	4	19.0	0	
Prefers to stay	14	87.5	0		2	12.5
Number of persons—120						

Ex-pastors were asked to rate the importance of 24 possible reasons for moving into secular employment (Table B22). One reason was "wife or family unhappy," to which 54.2 percent gave some degree of importance in their decisions. Nearly one third of these (16.8%) rated it high in importance. For 10 of the interviewed, it was the dominant reason for their move.

When we asked the ex-pastors how their wives felt about the decision to leave, we found that 54.9 percent of the men said their wives preferred or were eager to leave, 16.8 percent were neutral, and 12.2 percent preferred to stay (Table 31). A similar question asked of the pastors, concerning how their wives feel

Table 31. Wives' Feelings About Leaving Ministry

Wife's Feelings	EX-PASTORS (131)		PASTORS (250)		
	Number	Percent	Number	Percent	
Very reluctant to leave	3	2.3	87	34.8	Very eager to stay
Willing to leave but preferred to stay	13	9.9	84	33.6	Willing to leave but prefers to stay
Neutral	22	16.8	46	18.4	Neutral
Preferred to leave but willing to stay	49	37.4	15	6.0	Prefers to leave but willing to stay
Very eager to leave	23	17.5	3	1.2	Very eager to leave
No response	21	16.0	15	6.0	No response
	131	99.9	250	100.0	

about being in the ministry, brought reports of 68.4 percent preferring or eager to stay, 18.4 percent being neutral, and only 7.2 percent preferring to leave. These figures accurately reflect the fact that a minister's career decisions and his perception of his wife's feelings are very closely associated.

We felt that the wives' desire to leave might be strongly related to inadequate income, but apparently it is not (Table 32). Among those whose wives were ea-

Table 32. Wives' Feelings About Leaving, and Money as a Factor in the Decision

Wife's Feelings	MONEY AS A FACTOR IN THE DECISION					
	Very Much	Moderate	Not Much	None	Unknown	Total
Eager to leave (21)	4.8	9.5	4.8	71.4	9.5	100.0
Preferring to leave but willing to stay (49)	12.2	12.2	0	57.1	18.4	100.0
Neutral (22)	10.0	10.0	10.0	55.0	15.0	100.0
Preferring or eager to stay (16)	25.0	6.5	0	62.5	6.3	100.0
Number of persons—108						

ger to leave, 71.4 percent say that money had nothing to do with the decision, while only 4.8 percent report it as very much a factor. On the other hand, those whose wives preferred or were eager to stay, say money was very much a factor in 25 percent of the decisions, and had nothing to do with it in 62.5 percent of the decisions. A wife's eagerness to move seems not to be the result of money problems.

THE COERCIVE POWER OF MARITAL CRISES

It is already clear how career decisions are influenced by the minister's concern for his family's welfare and his wife's happiness. There is another, harsher impact of marriage on career, growing out of a crisis in the marriage relationship. Our data show that while this is not characteristic of most decisions to leave church employment, it is either a precipitating or a complicating factor for an important minority. Among the ex-pastors 11.8 percent are divorced or separated, whereas only 2.8 percent of the pastors report such marital crises (Table B10). A 1964 study of 390 UCC pastors showed only 2.2 percent divorced or separated.* Divorce and separation were the dominant reasons for leaving among 6.3 percent of our interviewed ex-pastors. Moreover, in reporting changes in family life since leaving, a fifth of the men had had severe family problems, most of which were in marital relationships; and an additional seventh reported milder pressures within the family, which were contributing causes of the move (Table B28).

That this is not unique to the United Church of Christ is shown by a study of United Presbyterian clergy (Mills, 1969), in which marital crisis was one of the principal reasons for moves into secular employment. Although several types of career moves were studied, separation and divorce were found only among those leaving church employment altogether.

Ex-pastors were asked, At the time you were making the decision to leave, was the relationship between you and your wife:
—warm and supportive?
—ambivalent and unpredictable?
—cool and distant?
—tending toward separation?
—separated or divorced?

Pastors were asked a similar question about the "present relationship between you and your wife." The tabulation of responses is given in Table 33. Although nearly three fourths of the ex-pastors report warm and supportive relationships, 15.8 percent report deteriorating marriages, as compared with less than 1 percent of the pastors.

The coercive power of marital crises is seen in the fact that of the eight whose dominant reason for leaving was divorce or separation, only two felt they could have remained as much as a year longer. By contrast, half of those whose dominant reason involved other types of family problems felt they could have stayed a year or more, and nearly two thirds (63.2%) of the others could have stayed a year or more (Table 34). Moreover, when asked the source of the *urgency* of their moves, family problems accounted for 9 of 33 who said they had to leave

---

* Unpublished data from clergy support study; see Scherer, 1964.

Table 33. Relationships Between Ministers and Wives

Husband-Wife Relationship	EX–PASTORS, WHEN DECIDING TO LEAVE CHURCH POSITION		PASTORS, AT PRESENT TIME	
	Number	Percent	Number	Percent
Warm and supportive	83	72.8	209	88.9
Ambivalent and unpredictable	11	9.6	22	9.4
Cool and distant	2	1.8	2	0.9
Tending toward separation	9	7.9	2	0.9
Separated or divorced	9	7.9	0	0
	114	100.0	235	100.1

Table 34. Dominant Reasons (Involving Family) and Degree of Urgency of Move

Dominant Reasons for Leaving, Involving Family	DEGREE OF URGENCY OF MOVE			
	Had to Leave Church or Ministry Immediately	Could Have Stayed Less Than a Year	Could Have Stayed a Year or More	Total
Problems of wife and children	6	2	8	16
Divorce or separation	3	3	2	8
Other reasons	24	11	60	95
	33	16	70	119

their churches immediately, but for only 10 of 70 who said they could have stayed a year or more (Table 15, p. 70).

It may seem that we have labored the point in showing the influence of family problems, but it appears that ex-pastors scarcely recognize the significance of their family systems in making career decisions. In the interviews we asked two questions which should have produced many references to family concerns. We asked, What would have had to be different for you to remain in church employment? Among the wide variety of answers, only five mentioned family matters, and all five referred to separation and divorce. Again we asked, What, in your opinion, is the biggest difference between ministers who stay and those who leave? Although the responses were varied and imaginative, *not one mentioned the effect of the minister's family relationships upon his decision.* Yet these are the same respondents who valued the praise of their wives above that of their work associates and close friends, who report their wives far more supportive than other reference persons, and whose professional life is intimately bound to the quality of their family relationships.

Without more information, we can only speculate on whether this silence stems from genuine lack of awareness or is due to a reluctance to acknowledge the role played by family influences. One can argue the latter, that it seemed inappropriate or unmanly to attribute career decisions to family concerns, but we incline toward the former as more likely. The sequence of interview questions and the general character of the queries encouraged the ex-pastor to consider many influences on his decision, and the family is included among them. Other relatively sensitive points were discussed rather freely by ex-pastors, and it seems likely that failure to mention this one is probably due to lack of awareness. In any case, it is a topic which merits intensive study, for the power of the family system to influence the minister's career decisions must be greatly enhanced by his ignorance of that power. This ignorance may well mark the difference between a healthy integration of work and family roles, on the one hand, and unhealthy dependence upon wife and family for the kinds of support and encouragement which others gain through their colleagues and constituency relationships.

Having described the influence of family on career decisions, at least two points should be made about reciprocal effects. First, the ministry is a strain even on a strong marriage. Thirty-two ex-pastors reporting warm and supportive wives when they were deciding to move also report that their marital relationships are happier *now,* even though this was not a factor in the decision (Table 35). There is a general quality of relaxation and freedom about much postpastorate life which apparently has a positive effect even in happy families.

Second, the interviews suggest that marriages are not usually saved by leaving church employment. Eleven out of 16 who reported marital crises when they left are now separated or divorced, and a twelfth reports his family situation "unhappier now." Three of 13 who had "ambivalent and unpredictable" or "cool and distant" marriages are also separated or divorced, and a fourth is "unhappier now." However, the other types of family problems, largely involving health problems, do seem to be considerably helped by the move. In fact, 29 report significant improvements in family problems which were contributing factors in career-change decisions, and only eight of these appear to be related to husband-wife conflict.

Changing Faith

The commitment to serve the Lord in the ministry is a faith commitment which is in some way the strongest basis of a pastor's occupational identity. Many speculations exist that serious loss or change of faith among clergymen account for a major portion of those leaving church ministries. Because there is much evidence of changing theologies but none concerning their impact on occupational commitment, and because the research team itself was divided in the hypotheses we favored on this topic, we built into the instruments several indi-

Table 35. Husband-Wife Relationships and Post-pastorate Changes in Family Life

Relationship at Time of Decision	Problems Were Not a Decision Factor but Family Is Happier Now	Problems Were a Factor and Are Improved Now	Problems Led to Divorce or Separation	No Change	Family Unhappier Now	Other
1 Warm and supportive	32	21	0	21	5	3
2–3 Ambivalent or distant	3	6	3	0	1	0
4–5 Tending toward or actually separated or divorced	0	2	11	1	1	1
	35	29	14	22	7	4
Number of persons—111						

cators of change or loss of faith. The net result is to confirm the steady liberalization and pragmatization of faith among the clergy, and to identify roots of these changes which differ somewhat between the ex-pastors and the pastors. Nevertheless, our findings give no encouragement to the view that loss of faith is responsible for moves into secular work. On the contrary, they suggest that enlarging and deepening faith provides major undergirding for the redefinition of self-concept and vocation undertaken by most ex-pastors to fit their radically changed occupational status.

The general changes in theological climate are revealed by three questionnaire items completed by the ex-pastors and pastors. A "theological triangle" was presented (see below), and respondents were asked to locate within the triangle their own theological views when they first entered the parish ministry

TRIANGULAR THEOLOGICAL FIELD

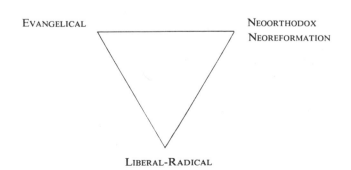

EVANGELICAL

NEOORTHODOX
NEOREFORMATION

LIBERAL-RADICAL

Table 36. Theological Position Held When Entering and Leaving Pastoral Ministry

	EX–PASTORS (126) (percent)		PASTORS (250) (percent)	
	WHEN ENTERING	WHEN LEAVING	WHEN ENTERING	NOW
Evangelical *	13.7	2.3	18.4	4.8
Neoorthodox or Neoreformation	35.1	23.7	39.6	26.8
Liberal-radical	29.0	47.3	21.2	41.2
Middle-of-road	9.2	9.2	12.8	19.2
No response	13.0	17.6	8.0	8.0

* General viewpoint identified with National Association of Evangelicals.

and then when they left for their present work. Table 36 shows that, although ex-pastors were slightly less conservative and more liberal when they entered as well as when they left, the same changes have occurred in both groups: neo-orthodoxy and conservatism have lost heavily while liberal views have gained. A similar finding was reported by McCune and Mills (1968) for Episcopal and Presbyterian clergy, although among Methodists liberalism lost adherents to neo-orthodoxy. A second aspect of theological change is suggested by the McCune-Mills finding that, in addition to a liberalizing movement, many men report more "tolerant" attitudes, caring less about technical theological points and being more open to many views. "These unstructured responses suggest that part of the movement away from conservatism is toward the acceptance of theological pluralism, while much of the remainder is toward a liberal theology" (p. 20).

A more complex question sought to identify the types of theological change and their frequency. From responses to open-ended questions in earlier studies, we defined 6 polarities and asked respondents to check statements which applied to them. Ex-pastors in particular were asked about the years preceding their move out of church employment. Table 37 shows the results. Fifty-five ex-pastors and 52 pastors reported there had been no significant change in their views. Seventy-six ex-pastors and 196 pastors checked 1 or more of the 12 statements defining the 6 theological polarities. In every category, more pastors than ex-pastors report change. The difference is particularly prominent in the first statement, "from theoretical to practical emphases," which describes 61.2 percent of the pastors but only 30.5 percent of the ex-pastors.

More significant than the differences, however, is the similarity of pattern in the responses. Both groups consistently chose statements reflecting changes toward pragmatic, liberal, humanistic, and tolerant views. Very few men reported moves toward more theoretical, more conservative, stricter, or more religious positions. The liberalizing and pragmatizing of faith has not gone hand in hand with doubt and uncertainty, however, since both groups described changes "from uncertain in faith to more deeply committed." They are rather evenly divided

Table 37. Changes in Theological Views in Recent Years *

| | EX–PASTORS (131) | | PASTORS (250) | |
CHANGES	NUMBER	PERCENT	NUMBER	PERCENT
From theoretical to practical emphases	40	30.5	153	61.2
From practical to theoretical emphases	4	3.1	9	3.6
From liberal to conservative theological doctrine	4	3.1	20	8.0
From conservative to liberal theological doctrine	24	18.3	62	24.8
From strictly religious to humanistic or ethical concerns	35	26.7	84	33.6
From humanistic or ethical to strictly religious concerns	1	0.8	11	4.4
From rather tolerant to rather strict views	2	1.8	7	2.8
From rather strict to rather tolerant views	33	25.2	105	42.0
From uncertain in faith to more deeply committed	27	20.6	71	28.4
From more deeply committed to uncertain in faith	10	7.6	26	10.4
From caring a lot about theology to caring very little about it	13	9.9	40	16.0
From caring very little about theology to caring a lot about it	9	6.9	45	18.0
There were no significant changes	55	42.0	52	20.8

* Ex-pastors were asked about "the years preceding your move out of church employment." Pastors were asked about "recent years."

over the relevance of theology, with some moving toward a new emphasis on theology and others moving away from it.

The most illuminating of the three items directed to the delineation of faith changes asked about "high importance of causes of recent changes in theological views." Thirteen possible causes were identified and a rating scale from 1 (unimportant) to 6 (extremely important) provided for responses. Table 38 reports the number of 5 and 6 ratings (extremely important) given by ex-pastors and pastors to each possible cause of change in their theological position. Although the 82 ex-pastors and 201 pastors who responded to this question agree that the most important cause of change has been "increasing maturity," they differ considerably on the relative importance of other sources of change. Ex-pastors give second and third importance to "participation in movements for social justice" and "urbanization and secularization in society." Pastors, on the other hand, list "pastoral experiences" and "closer contact with many kinds of people" as second

Table 38. High Importance of Causes of Recent Changes in Theological Views

	EX–PASTORS		PASTORS	
	NUMBER	PERCENT	NUMBER	PERCENT
Value changes in our culture	25	19.1	65	26.0
Pastoral experiences	32	24.4	150	60.0
Participation in movements for social justice	36	27.5	61	24 4
Rapid scientific and technological development	23	17.6	76	30.4
Your own increasing maturity	44	33.6	152	60.8
Study or discussion with peers	30	22.9	89	35.6
Urbanization and secularization in society	34	30.0	78	31.2
Personal conversion or very moving experience	4	3.1	27	10.8
Recent developments in the field of theology	7	5.3	40	16.0
Irrelevance of ministry to problems of world	32	24.4	66	26.4
Closer contact with many kinds of people	29	22.1	114	45.6
Influence of your wife and family	12	9.2	37	14.8
Formal continuing education	17	13.0	48	19.2
There were no significant changes *	49	37.4	39	15.6

* The fact that fewer "no significant changes" responses are given here than in Table 37 is due to the tendency of a few men to report here the reasons for subtle shifts in their views, shifts which they were unable to fit into the six theological polarities of Table 37 and thus reported these simply as "no significant changes."

and third in importance. These rather striking differences are somewhat ameliorated by the fact that pastoral experiences are fourth in importance for the ex-pastors and urbanization-secularization is fifth in importance for the pastors. Nevertheless, the lesson is plain: men leaving church employment report theological changes similar to those of pastors, but more frequently they consider the changes to have come through involvement with radical changes in society rather than through pastoral and personal involvement with people. This suggests that there is more than one route to the modernization of theology.

Even though fewer pastors attribute change to their involvement in social justice movements, 30.3 percent is still a substantial number. What happens to such men in the parish? Hadden (1969) points out the tendency of social activists to move into nonparish structures such as specialized ministries or denominational leadership positions. Is this the route ahead for many pastors? Or are they to stay committed to parish life with its pastoral experience and intimate contact with many kinds of people, even though the parish be bogged down in the status quo? Or is this 30 percent destined to become ex-pastors following the men we have studied intensively?

The "gathering storm" documented by Hadden is not contradicted by our data. His findings that clergy increasingly doubt the traditional doctrines is consistent with the movement of ex-pastors and pastors alike toward liberal, ethically concerned, and pragmatic views, often caring little about traditional theology but at the same time more deeply committed to the new shape of their faith. The sources of these changes also include those which Hadden suggests: involvement in social justice movements, the irrelevance of ministry to problems of the world, and the increasing urbanization and secularization of this society. Yet there are other major sources of change as well: pastoral experiences, the pastor's own increasing maturity, closer contact with many kinds of people, and study and discussion with peers. Changing theologies thus have their roots in parish experience as well as in social action, in reflection as well as in involvement.

One of the options chosen by young activist pastors is to enter action training programs such as the Urban Training Center (Chicago), the Clergy Internship in Urban Mental Health (Cleveland), or the Metropolitan Urban Service Training facility (New York). The trainees are largely drawn from clergy deeply involved in social change movements. Many of these men, however, balance social action with pastoral concerns, as shown by their ranking of 12 "things-to-do" (Winter and Mills, 1968). Eight months of action training tends to involve the men more in social change, and some show less emphasis on pastoral care afterward. Even so, as a group they show continued strong pastoral interest. Perhaps the key to renewal rather than attrition in the parish ministry is whether pastors can maintain this balance over the years.

If this is so, then the deepening chasm that Hadden correctly sees between lay and clergy definitions of faith, mission, and authority, need not lead to the total fracture of the church's life. If the changing patterns grow in part out of parish experiences shared by laity and clergy alike, then one strategy of healing will be to strengthen the shared experiences. In addition to wider lay involvement in movements for social justice, the laity should become more deeply engaged in the pastoral care of others, and in intimate encounter with many kinds of people. If these have been significant causes of change for clergy, increased lay involvement in them may well reduce the "confidence gap" between ministers and parishioners.

If the directions and causes of theological change are clear, their relationship to career decisions is not. For only one man was it possible to say that the dominant reason for his change was loss of faith, although 10 responded to interview probes by speaking of greater freedom to doubt, need for a new religious experience, or abandonment of the Christian God. When confronted with a list of possible reasons for moving into secular employment, only seven men gave high importance to "your own personal faith changed," but a total of 52 (39.6%) gave it *some* measure of importance in the decision (Table B22). The free church, relatively nondoctrinal character of the UCC may dilute the effect of theological change on clergy careers, an effect which might be much greater among groups with high emphasis on doctrinal orthodoxy.

Perhaps the best reconciliation of these bits of information was given by Gustafson (1963) in concluding that "adaptation" is the key to understanding the American clergyman's dilemma.

> The ancient must function under the conditions of modernity and under the conditions of a voluntary system, yet the clergy cannot simply seek modernity or be functional with reference to pragmatic criteria of judgment, for in so doing it loses its identity as the representative of a tradition that still has validity for religious men.

Theological change that comes by the successful adaptation of the ancient to the modern undergirds and supports the pastor's commitment to his occupation. But theological change arising from the rejection of tradition rather than its adaptation, even though it looks the same, will undermine the occupational commitment of the minister. It may still be Christian faith, but now that it is defined over against the institutional norms of church life, one of the results is redefinition of vocation, of ministry itself, as we see in the reports of the ex-pastors.

Faith, Vocation, and Self-concept

At the beginning of this chapter we set forth elements of two theories of career-change decisions. The first was essentially a sociological theory in which occupational commitment is sustained by a series of system involvements. The institutions and processes of society, the mutual commitment of professionals to one another and to their work organizations, the profoundly important expectations of family, and the articulation of a meaningful faith commitment all operate as guarantors of the minister's occupational continuity. In this and the previous chapter we have shown how these systems operate as support structures, and how strains within or between them create serious dilemmas for clergy. The effect is to weaken the social foundations of occupational commitment and to initiate a search for alternatives.

There remains, however, the question, Why do some ministers respond to system strains as challenges within the church structure, while others respond by career-change moves? To help answer this, the second theory, more psychological in character, discusses the balance of hope and frustration. Normally, dissatisfactions can be resolved or at least kept to a low level, and one's optimism about his work will render unimportant the residual dissatisfaction rooted in unresolved system strains. Dissonance between self and work roles is not terribly threatening so long as hope of remedy far outweighs the frustration of one's effort to change it. When the latter approaches the magnitude of the former, however, the balance of hope and frustration becomes delicate, because the normal dissonance-reducing procedures have been inadequate. The result is twofold: like a threatened animal, the aroused self begins to search for alternative positions in case the hope/frustration ratio further deteriorates, and at the same time one becomes vulnerable to experiences which formerly would have been manageable but now may act as "tipping points," precipitating a decision to leave the situation.

One of the implications of this study is that ex-pastors and pastors largely differ in that they live on opposite sides of the tipping point. As we have seen, pastors do not differ so much from ex-pastors in attitudes, beliefs, job dissatisfaction, role enjoyment, or even in search behavior—many pastors have explored secular employment. Pastors experience the same system pressures as ex-pastors, with the possible exception of marital discord. It seems likely that pastors differ primarily in still having hope that they can correct the causes of occupational dissonance. If this is so, then crucial support functions should be provided to help the minister in the nurture of hope and the management of frustration.

At the intersection of sociological and psychological theories of career-change decisions lies the *self-concept* as the integrative element in maintaining an occupational role. A person with a strong self-concept will, in fact, create his work role as a new synthesis of his own identity and the working situation he enters. In the ministry, which requires a high degree of commitment of its members, the prospect of entering a different kind of work can only be seriously entertained when his self-concept enlarges to include other roles. As the hope/frustration balance becomes precarious internally, and as his external system involvements provide less consistent support for his ministerial identity, he may respond in several ways: 1. With grim determination, he may redouble his efforts at church ministry in spite of it all. 2. He may depend more and more heavily on some system supports and withdraw from others (we suspect this is why ministers invest their wives with such powerful reference and support functions). 3. He may begin a search process for other work—a process which inevitably involves a redefinition of vocation (which for the minister is another name for his occupational self-concept).

Under the various pressures reflected in the list of dominant reasons for leaving—family problems, role frustration, inability to relocate, personal illness, financial burdens, and the attraction of a new career—one's vocation is thrown into question. Although few ex-pastors now describe themselves as having "left the ministry," no less than 73 (55.7%) ex-pastors attributed some importance to "uncertain of own vocation to ministry" as a reason for their move (Table B22). For 27 (20.6%) of them, it was a highly important reason. The effects can be seen in cross tabulations with responses to the task enjoyment questions. High enjoyment of role tasks is consistently associated with having few doubts about vocation, whereas low enjoyment is associated with strong vocational doubts. Moreover, those who seriously questioned their vocation also tend to have left because they felt personally inadequate to do the work or withstand the pressures. Those for whom inadequacy was *not* a problem tended not to have doubts about their vocations (Table 39). Also, vocational doubts were associated with a sense of hopelessness about improving the church situation. These pressures define the precarious balance of hope and frustration which initiates

Table 39. Uncertainty About Vocation as Related to Other Reasons for Leaving

| | IMPORTANCE OF: | | | | | | | |
| | SENSE OF INADEQUACY | | | | HOPELESSNESS ABOUT CHURCH | | | |
UNCERTAINTY ABOUT VOCATION	HIGH	MEDIUM	LOW	NONE	HIGH	MEDIUM	LOW	NONE
High	16	4	4	3	7	5	7	8
Medium	3	5	8	6	3	4	8	7
Low	3	3	10	8	4	7	8	5
None	3	7	9	39	8	11	11	28
Number of persons—131								

the search process and renders the minister vulnerable to a tipping point experience.

Again and again, both in group discussions and in interviews, ex-pastors would refer to their present work as "ministry," often more satisfying than the parish, or more precisely what they had originally felt called to do. It became apparent that the general movement away from systematic theological definitions and toward practical and action-oriented mission made it *easier* to redefine ministry as consistent with secular employment. In the first place, a de-theologized concept of mission harmonizes well with the new careers in social service and education most accessible to men leaving the parish ministry. Second, the use of pragmatic tests of mission rather than theological criteria allows many kinds of service functions to survive as "mission" even when stripped of all theological rationale and church location. Third, the massive confusion about the meaning of ordination is easily evaded, once theology is separated from mission-action. Finally, the steady shift away from traditional theological categories removes one of the few remaining barriers to the latent individualism in all American Protestants. Classical theology is strongly church-oriented, whereas much recent theological thought tends to be personalist or existentialist. Concepts of vocation based in the latter often come out highly individualistic. In the interviews, many ex-pastors voiced definitions of ministry which would have horrified them back in the days of their struggle against pious congregational individualism.

The redefinition of vocation and the reestablishment of one's self-concept as a minister even though not a pastor, provide needed continuity during the painful process of leaving church employment. The basis upon which this is done by most of the ex-pastors is a sustained, deepened, or renewed commitment to a more pragmatically and liberally defined Christian faith.

The Process of Decision-making

Exactly what stimulates a minister to consider other kinds of work and to begin the search process? How does he go about the search? How are his career decisions made? These questions are the agenda for the remainder of this chapter. Some answers have already been given and others are available in the grouped data from all the ex-pastors. But in order to see the decision process whole, we did an intensive analysis of more than one third of the cases, looking at their descriptions of how the search and decision processes were stimulated and carried out. Anticipating that the answers would differ by career stage, cases were chosen to represent clergy careers of less than 10, and more than 20, years. In all, 49 cases were analyzed, 13 from the older group and 36 from the younger.

March and Simon (1958) present a sophisticated discussion of the principal elements in "the decision to participate in an organization." In a general model of occupational movement, four mechanisms are involved: (1) visibility of alternatives, (2) propensity to search for alternatives, (3) level of satisfaction with the existing alternatives, (4) availability of acceptable alternatives to leaving the organization. The first and fourth of these mechanisms are essentially search questions, whereas the second and third have to do with the stimulus for search. We will begin with the latter, asking what the general themes are that initiate search and decision behavior among ex-pastors.

STIMULUS

This chapter and the previous one have pointed to many sources of dissatisfaction in the ministry and many ways in which occupational commitment is undermined by structural factors. Looking at it from the standpoint of the individual involved, there seem to be seven general themes in the experience of ex-pastors —themes which are woven together in their reports and which served to stimulate them to seek other work. The seven themes fall into three groups.

Noncommitment. 1. Never committed to church ministry. This theme stands by itself. If a young man takes a parish principally to see whether he's interested in that sort of work, or because he needs parish experience before moving on to a teaching post, we can scarcely speak of occupational commitment. In career development terms, the trial stage for some did not lead to establishment. In effect, then, this theme is not so much a stimulus to search as it is a reason why our decision-making models don't apply to some people. It is characteristic of the earliest years of ministry, appearing six times in our intensive analysis, always among men in the ministry less than five years.

Loss of confidence. 2. Personal or professional inadequacy. Some ministers lose confidence in their ability to perform well under pressure to achieve the kind of results they think important. This theme appeared 12 times in the 49 cases, all but one being in the first 9 years of their ministries.

3. General dissatisfaction and conflict—bad-fit problem. More often than any other theme, there appeared a characteristic story of growing dissatisfaction with the parish and generalized conflict over an extended period, leading the minister to the conclusion that he was just a "bad fit" in the pastorate. It occurs in 21 of the special analysis cases, nearly half of which were in the first four years of ministry.

4. Conflict centered around social action issues. A significant minority of min-

isters attempted issue-centered ministries which generated intense conflict within the churches they served. A frequent statement was: "The church wasn't interested in doing anything, so I decided to do my thing elsewhere." This appeared 7 times among the 49, 4 of which were in the ministries of shortest duration.

External pulls and pushes. 5. Personal crisis. The remaining three themes are loosely grouped as "external" stimuli to search behavior, since none is necessarily related to problems in the minister's work. Personal crises, of course, often grow out of work situations; but they constitute coercive pressures which are of a different order than those above. Marital, health, and financial crises are most commonly reported, along with one loss of faith. Thirteen instances arose among our 49 cases, not clustered by age.

6. Unable to relocate in a church position when necessary. With the sluggish placement system described in chapter 4, there would inevitably be cases where the system works too slowly for someone who needs to move. Of course, this is usually complicated by the reasons he must move or by characteristics which make him difficult to place; but the fact remains that this was a dominant reason for leaving church employment among 23 of the ex-pastors in the total sample, and as a theme it appeared 8 times in our intensive sample of 49.

7. Strong "pull" to secular job. This occurred only among five in the intensive sample, and as such is the least frequently encountered theme. In general, men were pushed rather than pulled out of church employment, although a few reported being offered such exciting jobs they couldn't turn them down.

One question which will throw light on the origins of the career-change process is, At what point in your ministry did you first seriously consider leaving church work? Interview records do not give entirely consistent answers to this question, some men interpreting it as "Under what conditions?" or "Why did you begin to look?" Nevertheless, our intensive analysis makes it clear that although the "gestation periods" range from 2 days to 15 years, most decisions to leave church employment are based on several years' consideration. Among the 19 who were in church jobs for 4 years or less, 7 had seriously considered leaving while in seminary, 1 while in graduate school, and 2 more had deliberated for at least a year. Men with 5 to 9 years of ministry and those with more than 20 years, report very few quick decisions; instead, they describe long years of wondering whether they should be in the ministry.

It seems likely that many ministers are in similar positions, reflecting from month to month on the desirability of remaining where they are, and vulnerable to tipping point experiences which upset the delicate balance of hope and frustration and precipitate a decision to leave. Some reports of tipping points seem almost trivial: a weekend spent mimeographing, reading Jonathan Edward's biography, an argument over a church budget. However, many of these critical moments were flashes of insight, and others were coercive events. One man realized he couldn't take the tension of parish life, another's wife became ill and the financial burdens were too great, another was turned down repeatedly when he sought to move to another church, and still another received an enticing job offer. The significance of the tipping point lies not in its content but in its timing, coinciding with the instability of an eroded commitment to the ministry.

Many aspects of this report imply that men now in church ministries may be as ripe for tipping points as those who have left, for example:

—The anger and frustration in pastors' counsel (chapter 1).

—The fact that 27.6 percent of pastors are very dissatisfied with the amount of family time available (Table 24, p. 80).

—Their high dissatisfaction with members' unwillingness to study and be trained (32.4%) or to carry out a Christian mission on the world (27.2%) (Table 19, p. 75).

—The commitment of only 37.6 percent to work "permanently in the pastorate" (Table B1).

—The report of a high degree of stress in the present jobs of 22 percent (Table B30).

These facts, along with the existence of the system problems analyzed in chapter 4 and the continuing growth of service and education professions, present a sobering outlook.

SEARCH

The search for other work follows several different channels. Ex-pastors for the most part found positions in 1 of 4 ways: an unsolicited job offer (9.9%), activity or entrée into another occupational system (25.9%), help from colleagues or friends (16.8%), and search through normal job-hunting channels (26.7%) (Table 40). With over half the new jobs coming either through con-

Table 40. How Ex-Pastors Found New Employment

APPROACH	NUMBER	PERCENT
Unsolicited offer	13	9.9
Activity or entrée into another occupational system	34	25.9
Help from colleagues or friends	22	16.8
Search through normal job-hunting channels	35	26.7
Other or don't know	27	20.6
	131	99.9

tacts in another system, help from colleagues or friends, or unsolicited offers, it is obvious that a well-connected minister will find it much easier to relocate. As March and Simon (1958, p. 100) put it, "The greater the number of perceived extra-organizational alternatives, the greater the perceived ease of movement." Just the process of turning down interesting possibilities is enough to raise one's dissatisfaction with his present work.

It stands to reason that ministers whose earlier careers have included secular employment of some sort might much more readily use old contacts and skills to facilitate their moves out of church employment. We know this is true in a general way by the analysis of career types. We assigned each of the ex-pastors and pastors to 1 of 3 career types depending on whether his job history began with ministerial work and continued in it unbroken, began with secular employment and moved later to an unbroken chain of clergy positions, or was an interrupted career with secular employment previously sandwiched between ministry positions.

Table 41 shows clearly that interrupted careers are more likely to appear among ex-pastors than pastors, whereas continuous ministries are more characteristic of those still in church employment. Several mechanisms serve to connect earlier secular employment with a higher probability of leaving church employment again. The remaining skills of an old role and the legitimacy of that role in the eyes of a dissatisfied minister would make him more ready to reenter it. Also, successful earlier career change may firm up the courage of one who is considering it in the present. Another important mechanism, is continuing contact with someone in another occupational system who knows that the minister has skills which are viable in that system.

In the intensive analysis, we found that about one third of the men with less than 10 years' clergy experience reentered secular work they had done before, but only 1 of the 13 men with more than 20 years' experience returned to an old role. Moreover, in analyzing the entire sample of ex-pastors, those under 40 are most likely to have found positions through connections with some other occupational system, or to have received an unsolicited job offer (Table 42). It is the men over 50 who are most likely to have gone job hunting by answering ads and visiting employment agencies. That makes the search process even more difficult for men of mature years who do not feel they can remain in church employment any longer, and it suggests that a priority concern should be the establishment of career-counseling and job-placement facilities for this group in particular.

DECISION

Finally, we sought to explore the decision process involved in these career changes. This proved to be the least rewarding and most elusive of topics. Although ministers are in the decision business, trying to engage their people in deciding to do what is right, loving, and true, they seem to find it difficult to analyze their own decision processes. Most of the decisions appear to have been made after years of deliberation, although 74 (56.5%) ex-pastors say a tipping point experience precipitated their decisions (Table 43). The periods of time required to reach a decision range from a few hours to many years, with no apparent consistency in reporting.

On the other hand, some of the decisions were made under extreme urgency: 33 (27.7%) felt they could not remain in their positions any longer, and another 16 (13.4%) would have had to leave in less than a year (Table 34, p. 99). These probably include the 39 men (29.8%) who left having little or no idea of what job they would take, and without even a good possibility (Table 44). Only 28 (21.4%) left with savings to tide them over the transition (Table 45). More than a fourth of the decisions thus are made suddenly and without adequate preparation. Without knowing in detail the causes of the urgency, it seems obvious that the church should not permit its pastors and their families

Table 41. Career Types of Ex-Pastors and Pastors

CAREER TYPE	EX-PASTORS (126) (percent)	PASTORS (250) (percent)
Continuous ministry	53.2	67.2
Secular beginnings	27.0	25.2
Interrupted ministry	15.1	6.8
No response	4.8	0.8
	100.1	100.0

Table 42. How Ex-Pastors Found New Employment, Analyzed by Age at Leaving

HOW NEW EMPLOYMENT WAS FOUND	AGE AT LEAVING					
	30–UNDER	31–40	41–50	51–OVER	TOTAL	
Unsolicited offer	20.8	5.7	13.2	6.3	(13)	10.6
Activity or entrée into another occupational system	20.8	35.8	20.0	18.7	(33)	26.9
Help from colleagues or friends	20.8	11.3	23.3	25.0	(22)	17.9
Search through normal job-hunting channels	12.5	30.2	36.7	25.0	(21)	27.6
Other or don't know	25.0	17.0	6.7	25.0	(21)	17.1
	100.0	100.0	100.0	100.0		100.0
Number of persons	(24)	(53)	(30)	(16)	(123)	

Table 43. Existence of a "Tipping Point" in Ex-Pastors' Career Decisions

WAS THERE A "TIPPING POINT" THAT PRECIPITATED YOUR DECISION TO LEAVE?	EX-PASTORS	
	NUMBER	PERCENT
Yes	74	56.5
No	45	34.4
Don't know	12	9.1
	131	100.0

Table 44. Job Prospects When Ex-Pastors Made Public Their Decisions to Leave

	EX–PASTORS	
JOB PROSPECTS WHEN MAKING PUBLIC HIS DECISION TO LEAVE	NUMBER	PERCENT
Knew definitely what job he would move to	69	52.7
Knew probably what job he would move to	13	9.9
Had one or more good possibilities	6	4.6
Had little or no idea what job he would move to	39	29.8
Other or no response	4	3.1
	131	100.1

Table 45. Financial Resources Available to Ex-Pastors When They Made Transition to Secular Work

	EX–PASTORS (131)	
FINANCIAL RESOURCES AVAILABLE	NUMBER	PERCENT *
Savings	28	21.4
Wife's earnings	15	11.4
Scholarship or parental aid	14	10.7
Other forms	40	30.5
No response	42	32.1

* Since several resources were available to some men, the percentages do not add to 100.

to be catapulted into such insecurity. While sudden departures may not be preventable, financial security, career counseling, and placement services surely can be made available for those who need them.

Making decisions can be done alone, but the advice of friends is often helpful. Most ex-pastors had close friends among lay leaders in their congregations (87%), among fellow UCC pastors (80.2%), and among ministers of other denominations (69.5%); but only about half sought the advice of these friends about leaving church employment (Table 46). With denominational executives, who carry considerable weight in the placement process, it was somewhat different. Only 55.7 percent of the ex-pastors had close friends among them, but 45 percent sought their advice. Ex-pastors also made use of close friends in their

Table 46. Close Friends of Ex-Pastors and Pastors and the Seeking of
Their Advice About Career Decisions

AMONG:	PERCENT HAVE CLOSE FRIENDS		PERCENT SEEK THEIR ADVICE *	
	EX-PASTORS (131)	PASTORS (250)	EX-PASTORS (131)	PASTORS (250)
Lay leaders in parish	87.0	88.0	43.5	68.4
UCC ministers	80.2	88.4	43.5	77.6
Ministers of other denominations	69.5	78.8	24.4	57.6
Denominational or ecumenical executives	55.7	71.6	45.0	69.2
Members of your present employing organization	35.1	N.A.	24.4	N.A.

* Ex-pastors were asked whether they sought their close friends' advice about "leaving church employment." Pastors were asked whether they *would* seek close friends' advice about "major career decisions."

present employing organization (35.1%), seeking advice in 24.4 percent of the cases.

The spectacle of having close friends but not consulting them about major life decisions is reminiscent of the old story about the little girl who liked parsnips but not well enough to eat them. Only in the case of the denominational executives and friends in the present place of employment—both of whom presumably could have been most influential in finding work—did a high percentage of men who had friends use their resources.

The analysis of career decision-making is a complex process requiring more sensitive techniques than we used in this study. What seems clear from our data is that for most men the ground for such a decision is prepared by years of reflection on whether the ministry is the right calling for them, that less than half the ministers call on the close friends they have among lay and clergy associates for advice in career decisions, that the most useful friends appear to be denominational executives, and that, in spite of all the friends, the years of reflection, and other resources, at least one fourth of the ex-pastors made sudden and ill-prepared decisions and moved out of church ministries into severe insecurity. One may call upon the image of Abraham who set out not knowing whither he was going; the foolish virgins, however, keep coming to mind.

Conclusion

We have presented both sociological and psychological approaches to the question, Why do some ministers change or withdraw their commitment to church ministries? By looking at both system strains and the hope/frustration balance, we have shown how a man is moved to adopt search behavior, to re-define his vocation, and to broaden his self-concept. This in turn makes him vul-nerable to tipping point experiences which precipitate a move into secular em-ployment.

In particular, we have stressed the opening of many inviting fields of secular work, the significance of the family in career decisions, the relation of faith to career continuity, and the evidence that many UCC pastors today strongly re-semble ex-pastors, except that they live on the opposite side of the tipping point.

6 / POLICY IMPLICATIONS

The intent of the research reported in this book is to take a careful look at a troublesome phenomenon in the system of the church—the withdrawal of many pastors from the parish ministry to take up work outside the institutional church. It is the purpose of this chapter to point up the policy implications emerging from the study. Although hunches and clues will be pointed to, the intent of the chapter is not so much to give answers as to shape the policy implications and formulate the problems which must be addressed by the policy-makers in the system of the church.

The world has changed in very radical ways and the local church cannot escape the major mandate upon every institution in this culture to update its style —this means the way in which the church speaks its message and the way in which it does its deeds. In an age when science and technology cause change in almost every aspect of life, in an age of managerial and communications revolution, in an age when all systems are being challenged and when philosophical and theological thinking are under attack, is it any wonder that there is trouble, too, in the system of the church?

Some in the church are aware of the crisis. Plenty of books have been written. We have heard about the suburban captivity of the churches, the aridity of our solemn assemblies, the shame of our comfortable pews, the gathering storm, and the crunch in the church.

One study of great merit and worthy of special attention is the World Council of Churches' study "The Missionary Structure of the Congregation" (*The Church for Others,* 1967). The study, which involves scholars, pastors, administrators, and practitioners from around the globe, clearly opened up the imperative concerning the reshaping of the local congregation of our time. It also moved toward this important consensus:

1. God's object of concern is the world, and the church is that part of the world where this concern is recognized and celebrated.

2. The world can only be understood historically as part of the transaction between God and the world. Men are involved in this historical process and are called upon to assume responsibility as partners with God.

3. The missionary call is a call for participation with God in his redemptive work in creation.

4. Christ provides signs of the fullness of humanity wherever men and women are led to restored relationships.

5. A servant church conducts its mission in the world through the corporate ministry of the laity.

6. In a pluriform world the Christian community will act through at least four types of structure: (a) family type, (b) permanent availability, (c) permanent community, (d) task force. Openness to the world and flexibility of structure are integral to this style.

Though this study is not as widely known as it ought to be in the whole church, nevertheless most major policy-makers and many pastors are aware of it. And among thousands who do not know the study there is agreement with the consensus. Signs that this is true are that many pastors and laymen committed to the point of view expressed in the study are both turned on by its truths and squashed by the system which they seek to serve. Many pastors and ex-pastors, as those reported in this study, have experienced in their lives the tension now in the church.

The signs are abundant that persons in the church most aware of change and most hooked on the future are at odds with a system which is failing to update fast enough. Some at odds with the church have quit; many remain. We will make a grave mistake if we ignore them, seeing them only as castoffs.

Since the inception of the study "The Missionary Structure of the Congregation," hundreds of books and thousands of articles have been written about the crisis in the church. But with abundance of data available, the signs are that the local church has not moved very far. Many have assumed that changes would come. Despite the yeoman effort on the part of some highly creative pastors and laymen, despite the heat put on seminary leaders and denominational judicatory staff, the local churches are all too often caught in the tight bonds of conformity and institutional self-service. With change everywhere, the local church is for some persons the last refuge from change and the one island of nonchange in a world where everything else is shifting. Here often the most conservative forces are in control. Here all too often persons allow the negative side of their ambivalence about change to have full play. Now it is increasingly clear that if movement is going to take place, it must be because leaders in all parts of the church's life lend their strength to the creative imagination of local church leaders who seek to update the style of the church.

The Choice Before Us

This study adds to the overwhelming data already available that the institutionalized means of gradual change is not rapid enough to keep up with the changes demanded of the church by the culture. Several options are now before us.

1. The churches can pull back into themselves, excluding all members, laity and clergy alike, who fail to adhere to the status quo. The current response in the Roman Catholic Church which excludes the priests and nuns who go against the birth control dictum, is indicative of such a strategy.

2. The church can use the cultural values of the world haphazardly. This strategy in which the church wholeheartedly embraces the cultural norms endangers the very real values of which it is guardian.

3. A third alternative before the church leaders is planned change. This entails looking at the trouble indicators in the system and attempting viable change. We advocate this last alternative and are hopeful that major policy-makers in the church will use the results of our research as a means of working at planned change.

The trouble indicator pointed to in this study of the ex-pastor is that of the loss of professionals in the church system. Important policy decisions are now called for in this time when the strong lines which divide us are not denominational lines but rather an orientation to the world and a perspective concerning the imperative of the church to help shape a new world being born.

The Systems Approach

Most of the policy changes needed point to ecumenical collaboration. Unless this option is taken seriously, everything else we do is going to be too little and too late. But we must make more than an ecumenical approach. We must also make a systems approach.

Pastors alone cannot solve the trouble in the church system relative to church professionals. They cannot pull themselves up by their bootstraps. Seminaries cannot solve it alone. Judicatories and church executives cannot solve it alone. If the problems are really going to be addressed and some solutions found, every part of the system must work together in problem-solving. This means that national and judicatory leaders, seminary policy-makers, and the most creative leaders of the local church must address the problems together and work out solutions. In this crisis of identity the church has a right to expect guidance from its leaders, and unilateral approaches will never be able to cope with the massive problems with any degree of effectiveness.

The policy issues which a systems approach needs to address are: (1) the need for role clarification, (2) the need for better support systems, and (3) the need for improved training for the pastoral ministry, the need for training in new skills. The remainder of this chapter deals with the related policy issues.

Policy Implications Relative to Role Conflict

This study provides abundant documentation concerning role confusion in the pastoral ministry. The pastor struggling and suffering with this problem must not be left to solve it alone. Many of the men who have dropped out of the pastoral ministry found the role confusion a burden too great to bear. It is our supposition that many more are considering dropping out, and they will unless help comes sure and swift.

Can policy-makers in the church system help the pastor in his role confusion? To whom shall he listen? The pastor carries on his professional career in the midst of mixed signals and conflicting expectations. The national leaders talk in terms of the local church existing for the sake of the world, and therefore of the imperative of the local church being essentially world oriented and deeply concerned about the problems of society. A subtle system rewards those who risk turning the local church even when that risk results in apparent institutional disaster. The judicatories closer to the local church give off mixed signals. They are more conscious of the need of institutional success, and keep the pastor's eyes focused on more money and more members but at the same time constantly feed him signals and models which suggest that institutional success is not what it is all about after all. This double kind of incongruent signal therefore contributes to the pastor's role confusion. The lay people in the church, eschewing sophisticated theology and sociology, just want a peaceful church to go to, conflict free—a place for comfort during the grinding routine and a place of refuge when crisis comes. And most of the laity bring the criteria for judging success (organizational maintenance) into the judgment of whether the clergyman is or is not doing a good job.

Which master shall he serve? Within his congregation are people of many different political persuasions; children, young people, middle-aged people; the politically active, the politically quiescent; the far-outs and the far-ins. Also present are the real estate agents and the poor; the business community with stakes in what is, and the social action group which wants to change everything. They all want something different of him, and in times of controversy they often feel themselves betrayed by their pastor.

Can he do what he really enjoys? While he was training in the seminary the pastor developed a mental picture of what his work was to be. It was an idealized portrait and if he was a good student, he very likely developed an academic model of the pastoral ministry. But when he took his first church, reality broke in and he found that he had to spend his time doing many things he never intended. Blizzard (1956) has described beautifully the dilemma of the minister being forced by external pressure to spend his time doing what he least values and feels least prepared to do as well. There are some things that he really likes to do. And the more time he spends at what he really enjoys, the more he feels conflict with the values of his constituency.

Can we help pastors with their own internal conflicts? The conflict within the clergyman himself is a very important arena. By internalizing mutually incompatible values and expectations, the minister creates a continuing struggle within himself relative to the satisfactory performance of his job. While in seminary he internalized the truth that the church exists for the sake of the world. The local church is to be "society problem centered." This involves massive amounts of the clergyman's time in the community. At the same time he has internalized the imperative of being the "shepherd of the flock." He wants to do both and is in serious tension because to do both well is almost impossible for him.

This problem is most surely a structural one, but it is also a problem which deals with the self-concept of the minister and with his own ability to resolve internal tension.

WHAT IS THE MEANING OF ORDINATION?

One of the critical questions emerging from this study is the meaning of ordination. Almost all the ministers in the study who have gone into secular employment want to maintain their ordination even while they are involved in such diversified tasks as social work, working as employees of the Office of Economic Opportunity, or selling insurance. These men now in secular employment force the question of the meaning of ordination. Though they are not the only reason for this reappraisal, they now represent a strong pressure.

For many years ordination has been essentially related to the local church and to those who serve in ecclesiastical judicatories. Now this kind of defining is thrown in doubt and the church is called upon to address this policy question.

In the June 1969 issue of *United Church Herald,* James O. Gilliom, pastor of Mercer Island United Church of Christ, Mercer Island, Washington, says:

> On rereading my own ordination vows (Evangelical and Reformed) and even those in *The Manual on the Ministry,* I am struck with how severely limited they seem. "To tend the flock of God" is not only questionable imagery for an urban society, but also doubtful theology. Every part of the services presupposes an *inordinately* pastoral and congregational ministry out of touch with the new realities of this mobile, complex, and sick world. I sympathize with the seminarians rebelling against the narrowness that seems to be the price of ordination. The ordination service should be both more general and more specific: more generally inclusive in its view of the representational ministries and more specifically inclusive of some kind of commissioning for specific forms of ministries that could change with the times.

One of our respondents urges:

> Redefine the ministry to mean professionally far more than that which is practiced in the pastoral setting so that it can be practiced in such areas as social work and still be recognized as a professional ministry. Why not ordain deacon physicians, nurses, lawyers, social workers, etc.? Let the ministry to the world be performed by those who labor to refashion, renew, or redeem human life in every professional sphere.

At the beginning of this study the supposition was strong that the ex-pastors had run out of faith and that the commitment of the minister to serve his Lord had eroded. Our study gives virtually no encouragement to this viewpoint.

Though there is little doubt that the respondents' faith is powerfully influenced by the events and movements of our time and that their concept of the meaning of commitment has shifted, nevertheless it is clear that for the vast majority both faith and commitment remain strong. Our study suggests that change of faith is not a significant element in occupational shift but is the major underlying stronghold of continuity in self-concept, providing a basis upon which a minister reconceives his calling to fit his radically changed occupational status.

In the light of the foregoing, this plea from another of the ex-pastors should surely be heard: "Continue to work toward a theology of the ministry which does not exclude a person who chooses to exercise his ministry outside ecclesial employment." Who will hear this plea? The theologians in our seminaries cannot do it alone. The pastors cannot do it alone. The judicatories and executives cannot do it alone. We must address this task together.

THE PROBLEM OF BEING A GENERALIST IN A SPECIALIZED AGE

In order to gain satisfaction from work, people increasingly need specialties. Law, medicine, engineering, sociology, economics, all have specialties so that knowledge and skills can be gained in greater depths. The clergyman is still trained as a generalist and is expected to be an expert in all areas, not only by his congregation but by himself. When he performs poorly in some area, his congregation complains about him, even though his performance may be superb in other areas. He often falls into the entrapment by agreeing with it and then feeling inadequate and angry.

Some attempts to correct this situation are being made in various seminaries. But considering the scope of the problem, very little is being done.

A drastic change in the structure of the local church will be necessary to satisfy certain needs of professional clergymen. Churches will have to band together and use a group ministry approach with each professional specializing for the most part.

Specialized counseling services can help a clergyman understand more fully his own particular talents and abilities, and even interests. But what is the good of it if the clergyman goes back to the old system which expects him to be a specialist in everything and equally competent in all?

If the necessary changes come, local churches will be required to accept a different form of clergy than before. In many hierarchies these changes might come through the power and authority of the hierarchy. In others, such as the United Church of Christ, the norms of the congregation will have to be changed accordingly.

A major hunch related to the problem of church generalists in an age of specialists is local church ecumenical planning or cluster planning. This is an idea whose time has come. Important research is now underway relative to viable models. Theodore Erickson, now on the staff of the United Church Board for Homeland Ministries, is devoting his entire attention to this emerging form, involving clergy cooperation and lay involvement in the planning of program and structure, and focused on mission in the local community. Mr. Erickson is himself a new sign: a member of a denominational staff but existing for the ecumene. His papers on "Cluster Development" are available for study by policy-makers.*

WHAT WILL WE DO ABOUT THE SMALL CHURCH?

Yet another major problem which exacerbates role conflict for the pastor is that of the small church. Most of the men in this study were caught up in the small church syndrome. Many of these small churches are unstrategically located now that the nation has changed from open country, small town, and small city to metropolis. They are also most likely to be provincial and difficult from a power structure point of view. Churches, just as persons, may become neurotic; and such churches may be pastor destroyers. They pay their pastor an abysmal salary and seek to keep him in an emotional and spiritual box. Furthermore, many of these churches are no longer effective and their institutional power should be joined to others. We have known this for a long time, and important movement will simply not take place until policy-makers in the church system become fully convinced of the serious danger we are in. Forward movement will not take place until the right signals are given from judicatories, and these signals are most often withheld by the middle management of the church.

Policy Implications Relative to Support Systems

The function of a support system within a profession is: (1) to set standards of behavior, (2) to provide a common reference group, (3) to provide a means of corporate action to keep the occupational system from taking advantage of the professional, and (4) to provide emotional support and encouragement.

The data of this study strongly support the assertion that some inherent weaknesses in the church keep it from being able to fill the occupational needs of the individual clergyman and that some aspects of the support system isolate rather than support the pastor in his work, and that still other aspects of the support system fail to function.

Here is a series of policy implications arising from this study relative to support systems.

THE PLACEMENT PROBLEM

There are strong data to indicate that many of the men dropped out simply because they could not endure the long time it took to get placed. During the conflict situations, most of them wanted to move and could not. This created a serious morale problem which led both to withdrawal and, in some cases, to cynical disgust.

An anachronistic and sluggish placement system is still operative. It is generally acknowledged that most denominational placement systems are little more

* For further information write to the Division of Evangelism, 287 Park Avenue South, New York, New York 10010.

than catalogs of men and women "available and willing" to move. Although a number of denominations, including the United Church of Christ, are involved in feasibility studies related to more effective systems, the fact remains that the participants in this study were subject to an old system and they quite rightly criticize it. It is hoped that this study may speed up the process of reconsidering this important aspect of the church system, and that policy-makers will understand that we do not have much time left.

The problem is a knotty one because the autonomy of the local church in many denominations militates against change; so also does the high competitiveness of the clergy and the church free-enterprise system which is operative. Yet we must face these questions:

1. How can we provide adequate support and evaluative structures for leadership during change periods?

2. How can we provide therapeutic support where needed during change periods?

3. How can we provide faster and more accurate placement for men and women who wish to move to a new position?

"More accurate placement" is an important phrase, for placement is not enough. Professional persons need placement in positions which maximize their strong points and minimize their weak ones.

How Can We Help When Trouble First Develops?

The first five years out of seminary are probably the most crucial in the development of the clergyman. For many of those who dropped out, the signs of trouble were apparent then. And in the light of their testimony, important signs show that the care structure for them was inadequate.

So long as the executives in the various judicatories hold the professional life of the clergyman in their hands, it is not likely that men in trouble will easily turn to them. Church executives must take seriously such questions as these and tighten up the concern for the church professional in the early years of his career.

What are the early warning signs of trouble?

Where can he turn for help?

What is the quality of the help he will get?

Many of the men mentioned a severe feeling of isolation. This is something like dying of thirst in a freshwater lake. What can we do to help pastors really support one another? While surely of great importance throughout one's professional career, the close fellowship of other pastors must be of especially great importance in the early years of ministry. We need to ask ourselves the question concerning what methods are now known or could be developed so that the kind of support needed could be given.

It is the conviction of the authors that the human-potential movement could supply important help for us here. The human-potential movement is just that, a movement. Its forebears are the small-group movement, the sensitivity-training movement, and now the important insights and methodologies of group therapy.

This movement has many centers and many researchers, but all are seeking to heighten human awareness and release human potential. What is already known by leaders of this movement about community building, support systems, and improving communication techniques could be utilized in the church and harnessed to help clergy give to each other and receive from each other that which they need.

The National Council of Churches' Division of Christian Life and Mission has authorized the development of an interreligious task force whose purpose is to relate to the research in this field and to translate the meanings into usable categories for the life of the church. There is important hope in this action, but it will come to nothing unless policy-makers throughout the church system are willing to make use of the data.

How Can We Help the Wife and Family of the Clergyman?

Data in the study indicate that during the process of dropping out, the ex-pastor puts an excessive load of responsibility on his wife and family. As other support systems fail, more and more pressure is put on those who are most intimately bound to him in the family.

For the pastor, his family and his occupational system are inextricably intertwined. This is both a beautiful truth and an important strength, and at the same time a debilitating weakness. This study has shown not only the great strains put upon the family, not only the exceedingly high importance of the wife's role in relation to the pastor, but also that pastors are not aware as they might be of the power of the family to influence career choice.

It is probably important for people in most occupations to maintain family stability, but for the minister his marital situation is decisive. There is considerable evidence both in this study and elsewhere that marital crisis and divorce represent nearly insurmountable obstacles to continuing in church positions, and that the quality of relationship between husband and wife and the attitudes of the wife have tremendous bearing upon the minister's performance and upon his persistence in church employment.

Despite the important place occupied by the pastor's wife and family, no denomination has a consistent program here, nor are most denominational staffs really equipped to be of great help. Most denominations have furtive and tentative probes at being of help, but the help is pitifully small and is usually not given until the family is in desperate trouble and deterioration has already set in. Is there anything denominational about the great need in this area? Why cannot denominations pool their resources and develop a ministry here in an area of great need?

How Can We Help Those Who Are Thinking of Quitting?

The greatest significance of this study may not be in the consideration of those who have already left the pastorate, but rather in the question of how many are thinking about leaving and what kind of ministry we will develop to help them. In a recent retreat held for pastors, someone suggested that those who had seriously thought about leaving during the past year should raise their hands. After the wisdom of following the suggestion had been debated, and after we had agreed that "seriously thought about leaving" meant that the pastor had discussed it several times with his wife and had begun to clarify options, we found that 38 out of 86 raised their hands. This is an alarming statistic.

It is clear that some stay who should not and that some leave who should not. But who is now going to help pastors in the decision-making process? Will we hold ecumenical conferences? Should we provide ecumenical services? Or are we going to stay in the same old denominational ruts in this time of great crisis?

To whom can these men turn in the process of decision-making? Is any help available? What are we now going to provide? The answer to these questions may well be the most important action emerging from this study.

The Career Development Council is a recently formed consortium of denominational staff concerned with career counseling. There is hope here that a national strategy may be developed for placing career development services for professional church workers throughout the country. But there is a vast shortage of money and specialized workers for this field, and policy-makers must hasten to address this problem with a seriousness which has been lacking heretofore.

Should We Develop Employment Services?

"I suggest that the national office establish a department whose specific task is to assist clergy dropouts to find suitable employment commensurate with their education and experience." This suggestion coming from one of our respondents has occurred also to others. As a matter of fact, there are already several agencies at work seeking to be of help. One such is "Bearings," which advertises itself as "a response to the distinctive needs of former professional religious, Protestant, Catholic, and Jewish; a young organization answering a new and growing problem; a tax-exempt, nonprofit organization." It continues in this way:

> *"Bearings" Offers a Variety of Services Tailored to Distinctive Needs*
> *Vocational counseling and job placement.* Over the past year hundreds of ex-religious have come to Bearings for vocational counseling, aptitude testing, job interview, and referral for placement. This often entails preparation of job résumés and counseling on interview procedure and techniques.
>
> *Group counseling with psychiatric social workers.* In the radical reorganization of their lives and the change in self-image that goes with it, group counseling among those in similar circumstances (some of whom have found their "bearings" in society) often is vitally important. The value of group experience of 20-year military veterans reentering civilian life is somewhat comparable.
>
> *Information seminars on financial and personal practicalities. . . .*
>
> *Housing information—costs and procedures.* Emergency housing in some cases.
>
> *Part-time paid professional consultants* in industrial psychology, psychiatry, and religious sociology.

The national headquarters of Bearings is 235 East 49th Street, New York, New York 10017. It does its work on a shoestring, and though it does work of great importance continues without adequate financial support.

How will the services be given in this area of need? Will we support such movements as Bearings, or shall we each go our own denominational way, once again not learning from one another and meeting the need only half way?

Should We Encourage Clergy Unions?

One pastor in our study calls out to his fellows: "Form a union! As long as we're available for two bits, laymen will regard us with subconscious contempt. Their self-respect is involved in the demands and rewards they offer us. A strike would be preferable to getting out as many have already done."

This kind of note was sounded by many in our study and though the idea still sounds radical, there is a growing openness to the formation of clergy unions.

We have already noted the poor personnel practices in many churches and the shabby treatment pastors sometimes receive. At present they are really at the mercy of the employing agency, and when the pastor is in trouble the judicatory representative is most likely to support the church against him. At best the pastor has only a "company union" to support him, and in many instances that is not much more than none at all.

The hierarchy is part of the clergyman's professional association. On the one hand it sets standards, listens to grievances, makes policy, supports new knowledge; and on the other hand it must be concerned with raising budgets, constructing buildings, saving money, keeping trouble-makers (even though they may be right) out of strategic jobs, and hiring personnel.

For clergymen to form an effective voice for setting standards, making policy, changing conditions or structure, they must be in control of some means of communication so that their side of the story can be heard. They need some organization which functions the same as a labor union or a professional association, where concerted action is possible. Our study reveals a clear need for pastors to increase their power. They are finding new power in the options which are now available to them in our society, and it means that the hiring organizations must examine more closely the needs of the clergy. Unless it meets these needs, we predict that in not too many years there will be a frightful loss of professional man-power in the church.

How Shall We Stay in Touch with Ex-Pastors?

Some of the ex-pastors are among the best minds in the church. We need them badly as consultants to the boards and agencies of our denominations.

Many persons in the church have not taken seriously the ex-pastor. Many who do get him into focus think of him in terms of betrayal, or they say, "He should never have gone into the ministry in the first place." However, instead of being betrayers, these ex-pastors feel that they have been betrayed by the church system which recruited them on flimsy grounds, trained them inadequately, placed them unwisely, gave them courage to preach prophetically, then proved unwilling or unable to help them when in trouble, and then let them go with scarcely an afterthought. We can easily become defensive and say that things are not that bad. But the feeling of pain and anger on the part of those who have dropped out is no more distorted than the abysmal attitudes taken toward them by others in the church system.

We have already shown how these men in leaving the institutional church ministry do not turn their backs upon the faith. Some of them want to get back in, many of them are willing to return to church employment under certain conditions, and only a few will have none of it. The step which the United Church Board for Homeland Ministries has taken in establishing contact and entering into dialogue is only a beginning. It is a very important step, but it must be followed by equally serious efforts to keep that dialogue open.

Perhaps the most important key to that dialogue is in the realm of experimental ministries. Experimental ministries have received the focus of attention in the church in recent years. High status has been attached to these "tentmakers," but it is just now beginning to dawn on most of us that hundreds of our ministers are engaged in secular employment and that a large number of them regard their work as a current form of ministry to which they are called.

Does it seem only romantic to speak of the probation officer or the insurance salesman or the welfare administrator as carrying out a ministry of Jesus Christ? Does this threaten the meaning of ordination? Even though it does, we need to reflect on the practical value of the situation. There is a deepening gulf growing in the church, across which it is increasingly difficult to communicate, a deepening crisis between laymen and ministers at the parish level, where there is a confidence gap and a loss of communication which is not improving. And where is there in the church a body of men and women fully experienced and knowledgeable in both—the role of the clergyman and the role of the lay employee in the secular world? It is the ex-pastors.

Someone once described the need of "bi-subcultural professionals" to help government officials communicate with the researchers whom they employ to answer problems, and vice versa. We suggest in this study that we have our bi-subcultural professions in the church and are ignoring them. It is not only the racehorses among them, either those few of outstanding ability whom everyone would like to have as consultants, but the large majority of ministers who are now in secular employment that constitute instruments of communication and reconciliation at the parish level.

No denomination has yet taken these ex-pastors with the seriousness they deserve. And we still await the time when an important movement in the country will link these men across denominational lines. When the church quits ignoring these ex-pastors and learns not only to undergird them but also to listen to them, an important forward step in the church will be made.

Policy Implications Related to Training and Retraining

In the radically changed world every major institution has had to rethink the training it gives its leaders and the retraining necessary for those who are already functioning in the system. Our study shows the church to be no exception for it has borne witness to the strong feeling on the part of the pastors and ex-pastors that they were inadequately trained in seminary and that they are now lacking the necessary skills for ministry today. A number of questions emerge in this area.

How Can We Make a Systems Approach to Recruitment, Training, and Hiring?

Under the present setup the recruiting system is separated from the training system, which, in turn, is separated from the hiring system. And even in many instances the hiring system is separated from the real constituency to be served. Young people choose the ministry with one set of ideals and occupational images, they are introduced to a radically different set in the seminaries, and when they emerge as neophyte ministers into local parishes they discover additional roles and obligations for which they were never trained. It is a well-nigh universal complaint among younger clergy that they had to learn to be ministers after they left the seminary. The young pastor discovers that the training system and the hiring system of the church are really out of touch. He is simply not trained to handle all the elements of his work when he actually gets on the job. And when we look carefully at the scene we see, too, that the training system simply does not exercise sufficient oversight so that it is able to have sufficient judgment about who should and who should not enter the parish ministry. To allow a person whose personality does not fit the parish ministry to enter that field is both a sin against that person and a sin against the church.

How Can the Seminary Help?

Sidney Skirvin of Union Theological Seminary was one of the interviewers of the subjects of this study. He participated in the Chicago consultation. After the conference he developed a very thoughtful report for his administrator. A portion of that report is included here to show the implications one man saw for his seminary program. He says the seminary must:

1. Give attention to the meaning of leadership in crisis. What does it mean that a minister is a change agent? Can a man be trained in seminary to be sensitive to these issues of change, and the dynamics of tension?

2. Continue to help its graduates evaluate as accurately as possible the potentiality which they bring to their work. This evaluation is being done at many levels, of course. At the placement level, we at Union are continually trying to refine our system of self-inventory to enable a person to leave the seminary with a useful perspective on himself.

3. Continue to wrestle with the issues of the ministry of the church in nonecclesial form.

4. Maintain sufficient contact with its alumni to be of service during crisis periods in the process of career development.

5. Above all, work toward the maintenance of a theological perspective available to students which enables them to endure and survive the crisis

of leadership without allowing their prophetic ideals to be ground to the dust of cynicism.

Training for the Pastor as Change Agent

In the above statement Dr. Skirvin sees the need that the present-day church leader be skilled as a change agent. There probably is no set of skills more important for the pastor in our time than that of being able to help the church as institution of change, to help people change, and to help release the human and other resources of the church for participation in the revolutionary events of our time. Besides being able to relate people to the biblical tradition, the modern pastor must be skilled in the planning field; be sophisticated about community power structure, role theory, organizational structure, community power; and be able to help his people face conflict in such a way that it will be creative rather than destructive.

Thus we have the question: *How can the recruitment system for the church professionals, the training system, and the judicatories of the church face more squarely the great need in the clergy profession for the development of new and necessary skills in change agentry?* And since there is nothing denominational about these necessary skills, how can we work together across interdenominational and even interreligious lines to see that the church leaders receive the skills which are needed?

Look at All the Lonely People

Much of the talk and writing today is rightly about the local church and the public arena, the church and public issues. Yet the church is hooked also to family life and is directly related to a man's private life where he struggles through the deep meanings and the deep feelings. The church talks about love more than anything else. It takes people on a head trip about love. It tells people that they should love; makes them feel guilty that they do not love properly, but it does not show them how. It does not help them develop the necessary muscles. Furthermore, clergymen are trained in the same way they seek to help people. They hear talk about love.

A not-so-ancient parable might illustrate our condition. Each week the villagers gathered to hear one of their leaders extol the virtues and benefits of playing the violin. He spoke with great eloquence of the joy which ensues, of the healing effects, and of the new strength given to those who play the violin. He also upbraided those who could not play. Each week the people came, each week they listened, and each week they went home feeling guilty that they could not play the violin, or if they could play, could only scratch out a feeble tune. The eloquent speaker did not offer to show them how; he just talked about it. Then one day to their dismay the villagers found out that the eloquent speaker did not know how to play the violin either.

Our culture is filled with lonely people, people in pain, people with great fear and anger. They come to church wistfully, longing that their needs be met; but too often instead of their needs being met, they are given words, "a stone instead of bread."

The end of the extended family in our culture has left a void which has not been filled. The local church could fill this void again if clergymen developed the necessary skills to call into being the kind of community which would fulfill at least in part the important functions formerly filled by the extended family. Now because most church leaders lack the skills for building strong, helping, loving community, important needs are going unmet.

It is not that these important skills are not known. They are. But the church up until now has failed to put them to adequate use. Involved here is the field of self-encounter, basic encounter, group therapy, and the set of skills now related to the human-potential movement. The church needs humbly to learn from those outside the church how to build community, how to sustain community, and how to allow the group, instead of the single big daddy, to minister to the person.

The respondents in our study, pastors and ex-pastors alike, testify that the seminary did not help them sufficiently in the field of self-encounter and that it failed to give them necessary skills in basic encounter. Certainly among the skills which are lacking are those in the area of loving and helping others to release their potential to give and receive love.

A Final Plea for the Ecumenical Approach

The problems uncovered in this study of the ex-pastor in the United Church of Christ are undoubtedly prevalent in every major denomination in this country. Here is a cluster of problems which does not know denominational barriers or the subtleties of creeds.

The problems pointed to here are massive. We are aware that the study has simply documented that of which many leaders were already aware. But awareness is not enough. What are we doing about the problems? Of course, all denominations are doing something. But the work is going on piecemeal.

We simply do not have time for such an approach anymore. The time is now here for bold new initiatives to be taken ecumenically. Both the planning and the training that are necessary need to be done by all who will work together. Even the structural problems involved must at length find their solution by the joining of forces. A lot of goodwill, keen minds, and millions of dollars will be needed to face the problems to which this study of the ex-pastor has pointed.

We think the principle is correct that denominations should not be doing anything separately that they can do together. We must apply this principle to the troublesome problems in the system of the church. The time has come to apply a systems approach to the long-neglected and dangerous situations in the clergy profession.

APPENDIX A / RESEARCH INSTRUMENTS

QUESTIONNAIRE FOR THE CLERGY IN NONECCLESIAL EMPLOYMENT *

SECTION A

We want to learn from the men who have withdrawn from the pastoral ministry to earn their living apart from the ecclesial institution. In May and June regional conferences will be held so that this disciplined listening may go on. But we ask you to begin the process now by filling in the following set of questions.

The first part of this questionnaire begins the process of learning from you. The second part will help us learn about you and is part of a large continuing effort to study career patterns.

Please answer as frankly and as fully as you will. Although your name is requested, the information will be treated confidentially. Your cooperation is appreciated.

PART I

1. From your experience in leaving ministerial work, what suggestions would you like to make to each of the following (use extra pages as needed):
   (1) The congregation (or other religious organization) whose employ you most recently left?

   (2) Your seminary?

   (3) Fellow pastors?

   (4) Laymen?

   (5) Church administrators (conference, association, national staff)?

   (6) Others?

2. Are there specific issues you would like to hear discussed in a conference of ministers who have taken up secular employment? If so, please list and describe them.

* First questionnaire, mailed with a letter of invitation, March 12, 1968.

Part II

3. Are you (check one): (1) [ ] Male? (2) [ ] Female?

4. Are you (check one): (1) [ ] Negro? (2) [ ] White? (3) [ ] Oriental? (4) [ ] Other?

5. Are you (check one):

(1) [ ] Married?   (5) [ ] Widowed and remarried?
(2) [ ] Widowed?   (6) [ ] Married and now separated?
(3) [ ] Divorced?   (7) [ ] Divorced and remarried?
(4) [ ] Unmarried?

6. If you were ever married, circle the number of children:

0   1   2   3   4   5   6   7   8   9   or more

7. The "time line" below shows six significant points in one's life. Please write your age in the box for *each point*.

	1	2	3	4	5	6
Your age:	[ ]	[ ]	[ ]	[ ]	[ ]	[ ]
At:	Confirmation or joining of church	Time of firm decision for ministry	Ordination	Beginning of first pastorate	Leaving last church position	Present time

8. Are there other highly significant events for understanding your career thus far? If so, please list:

(1) Event _____   (4) Your age then _____
(2) Event _____   (5) Your age then _____
(3) Event _____   (6) Your age then _____

9. When you were about 10 to 18 years of age, what was your father's occupation (check one)?

(1) [ ] Craftsman, foreman, operative
(2) [ ] Private household worker, laborer, service worker
(3) [ ] Clergyman
(4) [ ] Other professional worker
(5) [ ] Secretarial or clerical worker
(6) [ ] Farmer or farm manager
(7) [ ] Manager, official and proprietor, except farm
(8) [ ] Sales worker
(9) [ ] Other or does not apply because (write in) _____

10. When you were about 10 to 18 years of age, did you live most of the time in a community which was (check one):

(1) [ ] Under 2,500 (rural)?
(2) [ ] 2,500–9,999 (town)?
(3) [ ] 10,000–49,999 (small city)?
(4) [ ] 50,000 & over (metropolitan-suburban)?
(5) [ ] 50,000 & over (metropolitan-inner city)?
(6) [ ] 50,000 & over (other metropolitan)?

11. Denomination of your first church membership:

(1) _____

12. If any changes, give denomination and age:
    (1) Denomination _____   (4) Your age then _____
    (2) Denomination _____   (5) Your age then _____
    (3) Denomination _____   (6) Your age then _____

13. Your educational background (write in name of institution):

	(1) Degree	(2) Year	(3) Major field
(1) College			
(2) Seminary			
(3) Other			
(4) Other			

PART III

14. A work grid is listed below. Your "career path" is an extremely important part of this study. All, *full-time, nontemporary* employment is significant, *including* military service and secular work. Please provide the information requested in the grid as fully as possible about each position. The following instructions refer to the columns in the grid.

    (1) From your first position to the present one, in order, write in your title (associate pastor, church executive, chaplain, teacher, etc.) and if necessary, explain the nature of the position.

    (2) Write in the number of years served in each position.

    (3) Indicate approximate population of community by writing in the appropriate number:
        [1] Under 2,500 (rural)   [4] 50,000 & over (metropolitan-suburban)
        [2] 2,500–9,999 (town)   [5] 50,000 & over (metropolitan-inner city)
        [3] 10,000–49,999 (small city)   [6] 50,000 & over (other metropolitan)

    (4) For local church positions only, write in the appropriate number to indicate membership:
        [1] Under 150   [4] 600–899
        [2] 150–299   [5] 900–1,199
        [3] 300–599   [6] 1,200 & over

    (5) Write in the appropriate number to indicate (average) salary range (including housing allowance when applicable):
        [1] Under $4,000   [4] $8,000–9,999
        [2] $4,000–5,999   [5] $10,000–14,999
        [3] $6,000–7,999   [6] $15,000 & over

    (6) Please give an overall rating of your feeling of success or adequacy in each position by writing in a number from 1 through 6, with 1 for least or no success, 6 for most success, and 2, 3, 4, 5 for other degrees of success.

    (7) Please give an overall rating of your feeling about the amount of stress you personally felt in each position by writing in a number from 1 through 6, with 1 for least or no stress, 6 for most stress, and 2, 3, 4, 5 for other degrees of stress.

WORK GRID

	(1) Number & Title of Position	(2) Number of Years Served	(3) Size of Community	(4) Size of Church	(5) Salary Range	(6) Rating of Overall Success	(7) Rating of Overall Stress
1							
2							
3							
4							
5							
6							
7							
8							
9							
10							

PART IV

15. What field would you most likely have chosen had you not entered the ministry?
    (1) _____

16. When you went to the seminary, were you primarily (check one):
    (1) [ ] Seeking a *faith?*
    (2) [ ] Already a believer, and seeking a *vocation?*
    (3) [ ] Already clear about your vocation, and seeking to *prepare* for it?
    (4) [ ] Other (write in) _____

17. Do you regard yourself now as (check one):
    (1) [ ] Having left the ministry?
    (2) [ ] Still in the ministry but having left the pastorate?
    (3) [ ] Only temporarily out of the pastorate?
    (4) [ ] Other (write in) _____

18. In recent years, what two periodicals have most shaped your theological views?
    (1) _____
    (2) _____

19. What two periodicals have most shaped your views of public affairs?
    (1) _____
    (2) _____

20. What two thinkers have most shaped your own ideas?

(1) _____

(2) _____

21. In this triangular "theological field," please locate your own theological views by placing the following two symbols at the most appropriate spots:

(1) X = Your theological position when you first entered the parish ministry

(2) 0 = Your theological position when you left for your present work

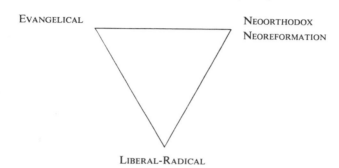

EVANGELICAL

NEOORTHODOX
NEOREFORMATION

LIBERAL-RADICAL

(N.B. "Evangelical" here designates the general viewpoint identified with the National Association of Evangelicals.)

22. If you cannot locate your theological position in this triangle, please indicate why (maybe you can help us improve it).

(1) _____

_____

23. Most of us appreciate receiving praise for work well done. During your pastorate, please indicate how much you would have valued the praise of each of the persons or groups listed below. In each case circle 1 for not at all, 6 for extremely much, or 2, 3, 4, 5 for other degrees of value.

	Not at all				Extremely much	
(1) Fellow pastors of same denomination	1	2	3	4	5	6
(2) Denominational executive who knew your work best	1	2	3	4	5	6
(3) Lay leaders in congregation	1	2	3	4	5	6
(4) Wife or husband	1	2	3	4	5	6
(5) Fellow pastors in churches of same community	1	2	3	4	5	6
(6) Others on your church staff (if any)	1	2	3	4	5	6
(7) Close friends not included above	1	2	3	4	5	6
Other individuals or groups (write in)						
(8) _____	1	2	3	4	5	6
(9) _____	1	2	3	4	5	6

24. Now you are asked to make a slightly different evaluation about these persons or groups: how supportive (helpful) they actually were and how much they tended to isolate or nullify your efforts as pastor. Be sure to circle the appropriate number for each person or group in *both* columns (1) and (2).

	(1) How Supportive?						(2) How Isolating?					
	Not at all					Ex- tremely much	Not at all					Ex- tremely much
(1) Fellow pastors of same denomination	1	2	3	4	5	6	1	2	3	4	5	6
(2) Denominational executive who knew your work best	1	2	3	4	5	6	1	2	3	4	5	6
(3) Lay leaders in congregation	1	2	3	4	5	6	1	2	3	4	5	6
(4) Wife or husband	1	2	3	4	5	6	1	2	3	4	5	6
(5) Fellow pastors in churches of same community	1	2	3	4	5	6	1	2	3	4	5	6
(6) Others on your church staff (if any)	1	2	3	4	5	6	1	2	3	4	5	6
(7) Close friends not included above	1	2	3	4	5	6	1	2	3	4	5	6
Other individuals or groups (write in)												
(8) _____	1	2	3	4	5	6	1	2	3	4	5	6
(9) _____	1	2	3	4	5	6	1	2	3	4	5	6

Your name _____

Present mailing address _____

_____

_____

Please look over your answers for completeness. Your cooperation is very much appreciated. Use the self-addressed, stamped envelope for mailing to:

The Department of Research
National Council of Churches
475 Riverside Drive—Room 834
New York, New York 10027

QUESTIONNAIRE FOR CLERGY IN NONECCLESIAL EMPLOYMENT *

SECTION B

In Section A, which you returned several weeks ago, you provided basic information about yourself and your ministry. During this conference you will be interviewed about the process of making the decision to leave church work.

Section B of the questionnaire completes the information about your experience as a minister.

Your comments are invited on any of the questions. Please answer them all as soon as possible.

1. When you entered nonchurch work, how did the move affect your financial circumstances?

   (1) _____ Much improvement
   (2) _____ Some improvement
   (3) _____ About the same
   (4) _____ Some loss
   (5) _____ Much loss

2. The following items refer to your most recent church position. Please respond by circling one of the numbers on the right. If your position was one in which an item was not relevant, check in the right-hand column.

How well satisfied were you with:	Very dissatisfied				Very satisfied		Not relevant
(1) Members' willingness to study and be trained?	1	2	3	4	5	6	_____
(2) Your own freedom to preach and to act as you saw fit?	1	2	3	4	5	6	_____
(3) The amount of time you had for family and private life?	1	2	3	4	5	6	_____
(4) The congregation's appreciation of your work?	1	2	3	4	5	6	_____
(5) The possibility that you could make a significant contribution to the vitality and mission of that organization?	1	2	3	4	5	6	_____
(6) Your salary and living arrangements?	1	2	3	4	5	6	_____
(7) Members' willingness to carry out their Christian witness in the world?	1	2	3	4	5	6	_____
(8) The opportunity to exert creative leadership and try out new ideas?	1	2	3	4	5	6	_____

* Second questionnaire, completed during regional conferences, May–June 1969.

	Very dis- satisfied				Very satisfied		Not relevant
(9) The degree to which laymen shared the leadership tasks of the church?	1	2	3	4	5	6	____
(10) The degree to which the work utilized your strengths rather than your weaknesses as a minister?	1	2	3	4	5	6	____

3. Ten role activities are listed below. Referring to your most recent church position, indicate on the right how much you usually *enjoyed* that activity, in the sense that you usually did it with enthusiasm.

	Disliked very much				Enjoyed very much		Not relevant
(1) Conducting board or committee meetings	1	2	3	4	5	6	____
(2) Personal counseling with individuals who have problems	1	2	3	4	5	6	____
(3) Serious study and writing	1	2	3	4	5	6	____
(4) Programming and arranging church group activities	1	2	3	4	5	6	____
(5) Helping individuals toward Christian decision and commitment	1	2	3	4	5	6	____
(6) Preaching (including sermon preparation)	1	2	3	4	5	6	____
(7) Leading in judicatory activities	1	2	3	4	5	6	____
(8) General calling in homes	1	2	3	4	5	6	____
(9) Teaching and training adults or youth (including lesson preparation)	1	2	3	4	5	6	____
(10) Giving community leadership on crucial social issues	1	2	3	4	5	6	____

4. In your most recent church position (a) did you have close friends in any of the following groups, and (b) did you seek the advice of those friends about leaving church employment?

	(a) Close Friend			(b) Seek their advice	
	None	One or two	Several	Yes	No
(1) Lay leaders in parish	____	____	____	____	____
(2) UCC ministers	____	____	____	____	____
(3) Ministers of other denominations	____	____	____	____	____
(4) Denominational or ecumenical executives	____	____	____	____	____
(5) Members of your present employing organization	____	____	____	____	____
(6) Others _____	____	____	____	____	____

5. Prior to leaving church employment, did you hold offices or give other major church leadership beyond the parish level? Please describe briefly.

Denominational: (1) Association:
(2) Conference:
(3) Other:

Ecumenical: (4) Local:
(5) Other:

6. How did your wife feel about the decision to leave the ministry?
   (1) _____ Very reluctant to leave
   (2) _____ Willing to leave but preferred to stay
   (3) _____ Neutral
   (4) _____ Preferred to leave but willing to stay
   (5) _____ Very eager to leave

7. At the time you were making the decision to leave, was the relationship between you and your wife
   (1) _____ Warm and supportive?
   (2) _____ Ambivalent and unpredictable?
   (3) _____ Cool and distant?
   (4) _____ Tending toward separation?
   (5) _____ Separated or divorced?

8. Here are some possible reasons for making a move. How important were these to you in leaving your last church position? (For each reason please circle 0 for no importance at all, 1 for least importance, 6 for most importance, or 2, 3, 4, 5 for other degrees of importance. Add other reasons which were important in your case.)

	Not important at all	Ranking of Importance Least					Most
(1) Inadequate salary or living arrangements	0	1	2	3	4	5	6
(2) Serious conflict with colleague(s) over job responsibilities or other matters	0	1	2	3	4	5	6
(3) Opportunity arose to do specialized work or training	0	1	2	3	4	5	6
(4) Wife or family unhappy	0	1	2	3	4	5	6
(5) Felt personal inadequacy as church leader	0	1	2	3	4	5	6
(6) Unable to relocate in ministry when move became necessary	0	1	2	3	4	5	6
(7) Family would greatly benefit by move	0	1	2	3	4	5	6
(8) Serious conflict with laymen over how to conduct church affairs	0	1	2	3	4	5	6
(9) Crisis in personal life made a move necessary	0	1	2	3	4	5	6
(10) Uncertain of own vocation to ministry	0	1	2	3	4	5	6
(11) Higher salary or fringe benefits offered	0	1	2	3	4	5	6
(12) Disillusioned with church's relevance to problems of modern world	0	1	2	3	4	5	6
(13) Health problems made a change necessary	0	1	2	3	4	5	6

	Not important at all	Ranking of Importance Least					Most
(14) Church coerced move by making things "too hot" for you	0	1	2	3	4	5	6
(15) Opportunity arose for larger ministry with greater responsibility	0	1	2	3	4	5	6
(16) Change coerced by denominational leadership	0	1	2	3	4	5	6
(17) Change was a planned step in a long-range career plan	0	1	2	3	4	5	6
(18) More desirable region or community	0	1	2	3	4	5	6
(19) Trouble *among* parishioners interfered with your ministry there	0	1	2	3	4	5	6
(20) To improve that church (or organization) seemed a hopeless task	0	1	2	3	4	5	6
(21) Your own personal faith changed	0	1	2	3	4	5	6
(22) Church did not take your leadership seriously	0	1	2	3	4	5	6
(23) Didn't enjoy the work of the pastorate	0	1	2	3	4	5	6
(24) Very attractive type of work offered	0	1	2	3	4	5	6

9. Below are several "From . . . to" statements illustrating possible changes in theological views. During the years preceding your move out of church employment, how did your theological views change?

Perhaps only one of these statements applies to you, or perhaps several do. For every statement which applies, place a check adjacent to it.

In the right-hand column you should also show the importance, if any, of these changes for understanding your career move. Opposite the most important change place the figure 1, opposite the next most important change the figure 2, and so on. Write 0 opposite all statements which are of no importance in understanding your move to secular work.

Statement of theological change	Change in the reverse direction	Importance for understanding career move
____ From theoretical to practical emphases	____ From practical to theoretical emphases	____
____ From liberal to conservative theological doctrine	____ From conservative to liberal theological doctrine	____
____ From strictly religious to humanistic or ethical concerns	____ From humanistic or ethical to strictly religious concerns	____
____ From rather tolerant to rather strict views	____ From rather strict to rather tolerant views	____
____ From uncertain in faith to more deeply committed	____ From more deeply committed to uncertain in faith	____
____ From caring a lot about theology to caring very little about it	____ From caring very little about theology to caring a lot about it	____

____ There were no significant changes

10. Were any of the following important as causes of the above changes in theological views? Please circle the number on the right which best represents the importance of each.

	Unimportant				Extremely important	
(1) Value changes in our culture	1	2	3	4	5	6
(2) Pastoral experiences	1	2	3	4	5	6
(3) Participation in movements for social justice	1	2	3	4	5	6
(4) Rapid scientific and technological development	1	2	3	4	5	6
(5) Your own increasing maturity	1	2	3	4	5	6
(6) Study or discussion with peers	1	2	3	4	5	6
(7) Urbanization and secularization in society	1	2	3	4	5	6
(8) Personal conversion or very moving experience	1	2	3	4	5	6
(9) Recent developments in the field of theology	1	2	3	4	5	6
(10) Irrelevance of ministry to problems of world	1	2	3	4	5	6
(11) Closer contact with many kinds of people	1	2	3	4	5	6
(12) Influence of your wife and family	1	2	3	4	5	6
(13) Formal continuing education	1	2	3	4	5	6
(14) Others _____	1	2	3	4	5	6
(15) _____ There were no significant changes						

11. Which one of the following best describes the urgency of your situation when you left church employment:
    (1) ____ Had no choice—could not have stayed in the ministry any longer
    (2) ____ Could have stayed in the ministry but had to leave that position immediately
    (3) ____ Could have stayed in that position awhile longer but less than a year
    (4) ____ Could have stayed in that position a year or more but not indefinitely
    (5) ____ Could have stayed indefinitely in that position

12. Was the *urgency* you just described:
    (1) ____ Due chiefly to your own feelings?
    (2) ____ Due chiefly to the pressures of others to get you out?
    (3) ____ Due chiefly to family problems?
    (4) ____ Other _____

13. When you made public your decision to leave your church position, did you:
    (1) ____ Know definitely what job you would move to?
    (2) ____ Know probably what job you would move to?
    (3) ____ Have one or more good possibility?
    (4) ____ Have little or no idea what job you would move to?

14. During that transition, what financial resources did you have to draw on, other than your earnings?
    (1) ____ Savings (approximate amount _____)
    (2) ____ Wife's earnings
    (3) ____ Scholarship or other grant aid
    (4) ____ Parental or other family aid
    (5) ____ Other _____

15. How do you feel about returning to the parish ministry at some future time?

    (1) _____ Eager to do so

    (2) _____ Would be equally happy there as in present work

    (3) _____ Am open to call under some conditions but prefer not to

    (4) _____ Definitely prefer not to

16. How about the possibility of reentering the ministry in some *nonparish* work?

    (1) _____ Eager to do so

    (2) _____ Would be equally happy there as in present work

    (3) _____ Am open to call under some conditions but prefer not to

    (4) _____ Definitely prefer not to

Conference _____
Respondent _____
Time at beginning _____
Time at end _____
Interviewer _____

INTERVIEW GUIDE *

UCC Study of Clergy in Secular Work

(To the interviewer: 1. The interview is divided into 3 parts with recommended time allotments. Please try to stay close to this rough schedule. 2. Keep your own comments to a *minimum*. Especially avoid interpreting the material or entering into dialogue before completing the interview guide.)

(Items marked * are optional. Omit if you are behind schedule.)

Begin: You have already given us considerable information about yourself on the advance questionnaire (refer to his so he is aware you have seen it). In the next hour I want to ask about your experience in church work and since leaving it.

I. Let's begin with your present situation (15 minutes).

1. At present, you are (recall his employment from bottom of grid, page 5 of questionnaire). Is that right?
(Probe: Be sure you know his position, his kind of work, and his organization.)

2. a. Are you still ordained?
b. If so, do you retain active status in your conference (or association)?
c. How long do you anticipate doing so?
d. What pastorate (or other church position) were you last in? (Be sure you get his position *and* organization.)

3. On the first questionnaire, question 17 asked how you regard your present status. You responded _____ (refer to No. 17 on yellow form). What is your feeling about that?

4. What difference has it made in your life to be in nonchurch work?
(1)

After first unstructured response, probe in following areas, if not mentioned:
(2) Job satisfaction:

(3) Relationships with other people:

(4) Feelings about self (self-image):

* Completed during regional conferences, May–June 1968.

(5) Marriage and family:

(6) Personal faith:

(7) Other areas:

II. Process of leaving (25 minutes):

Now I want to ask about the process by which you made up your mind to leave church employment and take a secular position.

  5. a. At what point in your ministry did you first seriously consider leaving church work?
      (Probe for the year, or the job, in which it arose as a serious possibility.)

  b. Why didn't you leave then? What kept you working at it?
      (Probe for specific reasons for staying in.)

  c. How long did it take you to come to the decision to leave?
      (Probe for "gestation period" of decision—whether process of leaving arose suddenly or reflects long-term or chronic problems.)

  6. Was there a crucial change, a "tipping point," that precipitated your decision to leave? If so, please describe the incident or situation that tipped the balance.

  7. What would have had to be different for you to have remained in church employment?

  8. When it seemed you might leave church work, how did you *begin* to look for other kinds of work?
      (Probe for how he began to develop possible alternatives.)

9. Who took the *initiative* in presenting your name for the position you finally accepted?
(Probe for role of church friends, nonchurch friends, peers, self.)

10. Why did you accept that position?
(Probe for whether the work attracted him out of the ministry.)

11. When you left your last pastorate (or other church position), why didn't you take *another* church position?
(Probe: What were your reasons for leaving church work altogether?)

*12. What, in your opinion, is the biggest difference between ministers who stay and those who leave?

*13. Have you noticed definite *stages* in the process of leaving the ministry? How would you define the stages of this process?

III. Now I'd like to ask about your experience in the ministry (20 minutes):

14. Do you now think you were well prepared for the ministry at ordination?
(Probe: In what areas was your preparation lacking?)

15. When you first entered the ministry, did you have any surprises? What were they? (Be specific.)

16. Conflict exists in many church groups, but in some it becomes so acute that it interferes with adequate ministry. Did you experience such a problem? If so, when (year or job)?
(Probe: If conflict was a problem, what was it about? You may want to ask for incidents in which he handled conflict well or poorly.)

17. How did you feel about administration in your church work?
(Probe for what he means by administration.)

18. Do you feel your marital situation influenced your decision to leave church work? If so, how?
(Probe gently for evidence of serious marital conflict at the time.)

19. How has your marital situation changed (if at all) since leaving the ministry?

20. Did you experience a major change in your personal faith or theology in the period before you left the pastorate/ministry?

    If yes: a. How did it originate?

              b. How do you feel it was related to your occupational decision?

21. Were there any emotional problems that affected your decision to move? If so, I'd like to hear about it.
(Probe for seriousness: mild, severe, requiring hospitalization)
(Probe for duration: long-standing, recent)

22. Finally, I would like to ask how your future looks to you now. What hopes and career plans have you?
(Probe for how definite they are, and whether the hopes include church ministry.)

PROFILE OF UNITED CHURCH OF CHRIST MINISTERS *

Earlier this year four hundred former UCC pastors, now in secular employment, were contacted. We wanted to find out what they are like and what they want to say to the church from their present vantage point. The majority of them completed a questionnaire similar to this, and many were interviewed.

Now we know a lot about former pastors and what they think, a lot more than we know about present UCC ministers. To remedy the situation and to make valid comparisons possible, we are asking four hundred active clergy to give us the same information about themselves and to offer advice to the church.

Please answer as frankly as you can. Your reply is anonymous and will be treated as grouped data. (The code number on this instrument is for purpose of follow-up mailings and a check on sample representativeness.) Only the final page will be seen by denominational leadership. Jud will see that your advice is taken seriously in New York, and Mills will process the remaining data in Washington.

Thanks for your help.

Gerald Jud, Board for Homeland Ministries
Edgar Mills, Ministry Studies Board

11/68

PART I

1. Are you (check one): (1) ＿＿ Male?　　　　　(2) ＿＿ Female?　　　　　(7)

2. Are you (check one): (1) ＿＿ Black (Negro)?　(2) ＿＿ White?　(3) ＿＿ Other?　(8)

3. Are you (check one):

(1) ＿＿ Married?　　　　　　　(5) ＿＿ Widowed and remarried?　(9)

(2) ＿＿ Widowed?　　　　　　　(6) ＿＿ Married and now separated?

(3) ＿＿ Divorced?　　　　　　　(7) ＿＿ Divorced and remarried?

(4) ＿＿ Unmarried?

4. If you were ever married, circle the number of children:　　　　(10)

0　1　2　3　4　5　6　7　8　9 or more

5. The "time line" below shows six significant points in one's life. Please write your age in the box for *each point*.

Your age:						
At:	Confirmation or joining of church (11–12)	Time of firm decision for ministry (13–14)	Ordination (15–16)	Beginning of first pastorate (17–18)	Most recent change of positions (19–20)	Present time (21–22)

(23–24) ＿＿＿＿＿
Do not　(25–26) ＿＿＿＿＿
write here (27–28) ＿＿＿＿＿
(29–30) ＿＿＿＿＿

* Comparison questionnaire, mailed to 452 active UCC ministers in November 1968.

6. Are there other highly significant events for understanding your career thus far? If so, please list:

(31) Event _____ (32–33) Your age then _____
(34) Event _____ (35–36) Your age then _____
(37) Event _____ (38–39) Your age then _____

7. When you were about 10 to 18 years of age, what was your father's occupation (check one)? (40)

(1) ____ Craftsman, foreman, operative
(2) ____ Private household worker, laborer, service worker
(3) ____ Clergyman
(4) ____ Other professional worker
(5) ____ Secretarial or clerical worker
(6) ____ Farmer or farm manager
(7) ____ Manager, official and proprietor, except farm
(8) ____ Sales worker
(9) ____ Other or does not apply because (write in) _____

8. When you were about 10 to 18 years of age, did you live most of the time in a community which was (check one): (41)

(1) ____ Under 2,500 (rural)?
(2) ____ 2,500–9,999 (town)?
(3) ____ 10,000–49,000 (small city)?
(4) ____ 50,000 & over (metropolitan-suburban)?
(5) ____ 50,000 & over (metropolitan-inner city)?
(6) ____ 50,000 & over (other metropolitan)?

9. Denomination of your first church membership (check one): (42)

____ (1) UCC ____ (5) Lutheran bodies
____ (2) Congregational Church ____ (6) Presbyterian and Reformed bodies
____ (3) Evangelical and Reformed ____ (7) Methodist and EUB
____ (4) Baptist bodies ____ (8) All others

10. If any changes, give denomination and age:

Denomination you changed to: Your age then: (43) _____
  (44–45) ____
____ (1) UCC _____ (46) _____
____ (2) Congregational Church _____ (47–48) ____
____ (3) Evangelical and Reformed _____ (49) _____
____ (4) Baptist bodies _____ (50–51) ____
____ (5) Lutheran bodies _____
____ (6) Presbyterian and Reformed bodies _____
____ (7) Methodist and EUB _____
____ (8) All others _____

11. Your educational background:

College from which you graduated: (52) ____
  (53) ____

____ (1) Elmhurst ____ (3) Oberlin College
____ (2) Lakeland ____ (4) Ursinus

_____ (5) Yankton

_____ (6) Heidelberg

_____ (7) Other UCC-related college

_____ (8) State or city college or university

_____ (9) Private, non-UCC church-related,
and other schools

_____ (10) Beloit

_____ (11) Carleton

_____ (12) Defiance

_____ (13) Doane

_____ (14) Franklin & Marshall

_____ (15) Pacific University

_____ (16) Did not graduate from college

Year: _____ (54–55)

Major college field: (56)

_____ (1) Natural science & math

_____ (2) Social science

_____ (3) Humanities (including history)

_____ (4) Religion

_____ (5) Engineering and technical

_____ (6) Social work, counseling

_____ (7) Education

_____ (8) Other _____

Seminary from which you graduated: (57–58)

_____ (1) Andover Newton Theol. Sem.

_____ (2) Bangor Theol. Sem.

_____ (3) Chicago Theol. Sem.

_____ (4) Eden Theol. Sem.

_____ (5) Hartford

_____ (6) Harvard

_____ (7) Lancaster Theol. Sem.

_____ (8) Oberlin

_____ (9) Pacific School of Religion

_____ (10) Union (NY)

_____ (11) Yale Divinity

_____ (12) Yankton School of Theol.

_____ (13) United Theol. Sem. of Twin Cities   Year: _____ (60–61)

_____ (14) Baptist Seminary

_____ (15) Lutheran Seminary

_____ (16) Presbyterian and Reformed Seminary

_____ (17) Methodist and EUB Seminary

_____ (18) Other denomination seminary

_____ (19) Inter- or nondenom. seminary

_____ (20) Did not graduate from seminary

Advanced study: (63)

_____ (1) Theological school

_____ (2) State or city college or university

_____ (3) Private, church-related, or other college or university

_____ (4) Other institution

Degree: (64)

___ (1) A.B. and other bachelor
___ (2) B.D. and other first divinity
___ (3) M.A. and other master's
___ (4) Ph.D. and other doctorate
___ (5) Other

Year: _____ (65–66)

Major field: (67)

___ (1) Natural science and math
___ (2) Social science
___ (3) Humanities (including history)
___ (4) Religion
___ (5) Engineering and technical
___ (6) Social work, counseling
___ (7) Education
___ (8) Other: _____

PART II

12. A work grid is listed below. Your "career path" is an extremely important part of this study. All *full-time*, *nontemporary* employment is significant, *including* military service and secular work. Please provide the information requested in the grid as fully as possible about each position. The following instructions refer to the columns in the grid.

   (1) Beginning with your present position and going backward in time, write in your job title (associate pastor, public schoolteacher, church executive, hospital chaplain, etc.) and the organization. If necessary, explain the nature of the position.

   (2) Write in the number of years served in each position.

   (3) Indicate approximate population by writing in the appropriate number:
   [1] Under 2,500 (rural)   [4] 50,000 & over (metropolitan-suburban)
   [2] 2,500–9,999 (town)   [5] 50,000 & over (metropolitan-inner city)
   [3] 10,000–49,999 (small city)   [6] 50,000 & over (other metropolitan)

   (4) For local church positions only, write in the appropriate number to indicate membership.
   [1] Under 150   [4] 600–899
   [2] 150–299   [5] 900–1,199
   [3] 300–599   [6] 1,200 & over

   (5) Write in the appropriate number to indicate (average) salary range (including housing allowance when applicable):
   [1] Under $4,000   [4] $8,000–9,999
   [2] $4,000–5,999   [5] $10,000–14,999
   [3] $6,000–7,999   [6] $15,000 & over

   (6) Please give an overall rating of your feeling of success or adequacy in each position by writing in a number from 1 through 6, with 1 for least or no success, 6 for most success, and 2, 3, 4, 5 for other degrees of success.

   (7) Please give an overall rating of your feeling about the amount of stress you personally felt in each position by writing in a number from 1 through 6, with 1 for least or no stress, 6 for most stress, and 2, 3, 4, 5 for other degrees of stress.

Work Grid

(Card II)

(1) Job Title & Organization (Begin with Present Job)	(2) Number of Years Served	(3) Size of Community	(4) Size of Church	(5) Salary Range	(6) Rating of Overall Success	(7) Rating of Overall Stress
1						(7–15)
2						(16–24)
3						(25–33)
4						(34–42)
5						(43–51)
6						(52–60)
7						(61–69)
8						(70–78)
9						(7–15)
10						(16–24)

(Card III)

(25 _____)   (26 _____)   (27 _____)   (28 _____)   (29 _____)

PART III

13. What field would you most likely have chosen had you not entered the ministry?   (30)
    ____ (1) Medicine   ____ (6) Law, criminology
    ____ (2) Social work, counseling   ____ (7) Armed services
    ____ (3) Teaching, mathematics   ____ (8) Music, theater, radio, television
    ____ (4) Newspapers, writing   ____ (9) Own business
    ____ (5) Engineering

14. When you went to the seminary, were you primarily (check one):
    (1) ____ Seeking a *faith?*
    (2) ____ Already a believer, and seeking a *vocation?*
    (3) ____ Already clear about your vocation, and seeking to *prepare* for it?
    (4) ____ Other (write in) _____ (31)

15. Do you regard yourself now as (check one):   (32)
    (1) ____ Permanently in the pastorate?
    (2) ____ Permanently in the ministry but not committed to staying in the pastorate?
    (3) ____ Planning on a specific nonparish ministry? (What and when? _____)

(4) ____ Expecting to enter secular work? (What and when? _____)

(5) ____ Other: _____

16. In recent years, what two periodicals have most shaped your theological views?

(1) _____ (33–34)

(2) _____ (35–36)

17. What two periodicals have most shaped your views of public affairs?

(1) _____ (37–38)

(2) _____ (39–40)

18. What two thinkers have most shaped your own ideas?

(1) _____ (41–42)

(2) _____ (43–44)

19. In this triangular "theological field," please locate your own theological views by placing the following two symbols at the most appropriate spots:

(1) X = Your theological position when you first entered the parish ministry (45) ____

(2) 0 = Your present theological position (46) ____

EVANGELICAL NEOORTHODOX NEOREFORMATION

LIBERAL-RADICAL

(N.B. "Evangelical" here designates the general viewpoint identified with the National Association of Evangelicals.)

20. If you cannot locate your theological position in this triangle, please indicate why (maybe you can help us improve it).

(1) _____

_____ (47)

21. Most of us appreciate receiving praise for work well done. Please indicate how much you value the praise of each of the persons or groups listed below. In each case circle 1 for not at all, 6 for extremely much, or 2, 3, 4, 5 for other degrees of value. (If not now a pastor, refer to your most recent pastorate.)

	Not at all				Extremely much		
(1) Fellow pastors of same denomination	1	2	3	4	5	6	(48)
(2) Denominational executive who knows your work best	1	2	3	4	5	6	(49)
(3) Lay leaders in congregation	1	2	3	4	5	6	(50)
(4) Wife or husband	1	2	3	4	5	6	(51)
(5) Fellow pastors in churches of same community	1	2	3	4	5	6	(52)
(6) Others on your church staff (if any)	1	2	3	4	5	6	(53)
(7) Close friends not included above	1	2	3	4	5	6	(54)

Other individuals or groups (write in)

(8) _____ 1 2 3 4 5 6 (55)

(9) _____ 1 2 3 4 5 6 (56)

22. Now you are asked to make a slightly different evaluation about these persons or groups: how supportive (helpful) they actually are (were) and how much they tend to isolate or nullify your efforts as pastor. Be sure to circle the appropriate number for each person or group in *both* columns (1) and (2).

(1)		(2)
How Supportive?		How Isolating?
Not at all — Extremely much		Not at all — Extremely much

Supportive		Isolating
1 2 3 4 5 6	(1) Fellow pastors of same denomination	1 2 3 4 5 6 (57, 66)
1 2 3 4 5 6	(2) Denominational executive who knows your work best	1 2 3 4 5 6 (58, 67)
1 2 3 4 5 6	(3) Lay leaders in congregation	1 2 3 4 5 6 (59, 68)
1 2 3 4 5 6	(4) Wife or husband	1 2 3 4 5 6 (60, 69)
1 2 3 4 5 6	(5) Fellow pastors in churches of same community	1 2 3 4 5 6 (61, 70)
1 2 3 4 5 6	(6) Others on your church staff (if any)	1 2 3 4 5 6 (62, 71)
1 2 3 4 5 6	(7) Close friends not included above	1 2 3 4 5 6 (63, 72)
	Other individuals or groups (write in)	
1 2 3 4 5 6	(8) _____	1 2 3 4 5 6 (64, 73)
1 2 3 4 5 6	(9) _____	1 2 3 4 5 6 (65, 74)

PART IV

23. The following items refer to your current pastorate (or most recent if you are not now a pastor). Please respond by circling one of the numbers on the right. If your position is one for which an item is not relevant, check in the right-hand column.

How well satisfied are you with:	Very dis-satisfied	Very satisfied	Not relevant	(Card IV)
(1) Members' willingness to study and be trained?	1 2 3 4	5 6	_____	(8)
(2) Your own freedom to preach and act as you see fit?	1 2 3 4	5 6	_____	(9)
(3) The amount of time you have for family and private life?	1 2 3 4	5 6	_____	(10)
(4) The congregation's appreciation of your work?	1 2 3 4	5 6	_____	(11)
(5) The possibility that you can make a significant contribution to the vitality and mission of that organization?	1 2 3 4	5 6	_____	(12)
(6) Your salary and living arrangements?	1 2 3 4	5 6	_____	(13)

(7) Members' willingness to carry out their Christian witness in the world?   1   2   3   4   5   6 _____ (14)

(8) The opportunity to exert creative leadership and try out new ideas?   1   2   3   4   5   6 _____ (15)

(9) The degree to which laymen share the leadership tasks of the church?   1   2   3   4   5   6 _____ (16)

(10) The degree to which the work utilizes your strengths rather than your weaknesses as a minister?   1   2   3   4   5   6 _____ (17)

24. Ten role activities are listed below. Referring to your current pastorate (or most recent, if not now a pastor), indicate on the right how much you usually *enjoy* that activity, in the sense that you usually do it with enthusiasm.

	Dislike very much	Enjoy very much	Not relevant	
(1) Conducting board or committee meetings	1 2 3	4 5 6	_____	(18)
(2) Personal counseling with individuals who have problems	1 2 3	4 5 6	_____	(19)
(3) Serious study and writing	1 2 3	4 5 6	_____	(20)
(4) Programming and arranging church group activities	1 2 3	4 5 6	_____	(21)
(5) Helping individuals toward Christian decisions and commitment	1 2 3	4 5 6	_____	(22)
(6) Preaching (including sermon preparation)	1 2 3	4 5 6	_____	(23)
(7) Leading in judicatory activities	1 2 3	4 5 6	_____	(24)
(8) General calling in homes	1 2 3	4 5 6	_____	(25)
(9) Teaching and training adults or youth (including lesson preparation)	1 2 3	4 5 6	_____	(26)
(10) Giving community leadership on crucial social issues	1 2 3	4 5 6	_____	(27)

25. In your current position (or most recent, if not a pastor): (a) Do you have close friends in any of the following groups, and (b) Would you seek the advice of those friends about major career decisions?

	(a) Have close friend			(b) Seek their advice		
	None	One or Two	Several	Yes	No	
(1) Lay leaders in parish	_____	_____	_____	_____	_____	(28–29)
(2) UCC ministers	_____	_____	_____	_____	_____	(30–31)

(3) Ministers of other de-
nominations   ____ ____ ____   ____ ____ (32–33)

(4) Denominational or
ecumenical executives ____ ____ ____   ____ ____ (34–35)

(5) Others _____

_____ ____ ____ ____   ____ ____ (36–37)

(6) Others _____

_____ ____ ____ ____   ____ ____ (38–39)

26. What offices or other major church leadership positions do you hold beyond the parish level? Please describe briefly.

Denominational: (1) Association (40)

               (2) Conference (41)

               (3) Other (42)

Ecumenical: (4) Local (43)

               (5) Other (44)

27. How does your wife feel about your being in the ministry (check one)? (45)

(1) ____ Very eager to stay in the ministry

(2) ____ Willing to leave but prefers to stay

(3) ____ Neutral

(4) ____ Prefers to leave but willing to stay

(5) ____ Very eager to leave ministry

28. Which one of the following best describes the present relationship between you and your wife? (46)

(1) ____ Warm and supportive

(2) ____ Ambivalent and unpredictable

(3) ____ Cool and distant

(4) ____ Tending toward separation

(5) ____ Separated or divorced

29. Below are several "From . . . to" statements illustrating possible changes in theological views. During recent years, how have your theological views changed? Perhaps only one of these statements applies to you, or perhaps several do. For every statement which applies, place a check adjacent to it. In the *right-hand* column you should also show the importance, if any, of these changes for understanding the direction your career is moving. Opposite the most important change place the figure 1, opposite the next most important change the figure 2, and so on. Write 0 opposite all statements that are of no importance in understanding the direction in which your career is moving.

Statement of theological change	Change in the reverse direction	Importance for understanding career movement	
____ From theoretical to practical emphases	____ From practical to theoretical emphases	_____	(7–8)
____ From liberal to conservative theological doctrine	____ From conservative to liberal theological doctrine	_____	(9–10)
____ From strictly religious to humanistic or ethical concerns	____ From humanistic or ethical to strictly religious concerns	_____	(11–12)

_____ From rather tolerant   _____ From rather strict to
     to rather strict views   rather tolerant views   _____   (13–14)

_____ From uncertain in   _____ From more deeply
     faith to more deeply   committed to uncer-
     committed   tain in faith   _____   (15–16)

_____ From caring a lot   _____ From caring very little
     about theology to car-   about theology to car-
     ing very little about it   ing a lot about it   _____   (17–18)

                _____ There have been no significant changes   (19)

30. Were any of the following important as *causes* of recent changes in your theological views? Please circle the number on the right which best represents the importance of each.

	Un-important			Extremely important			
(1) Value changes in our culture	1	2	3	4	5	6	(20)
(2) Pastoral experiences	1	2	3	4	5	6	(21)
(3) Participation in movements for social justice	1	2	3	4	5	6	(22)
(4) Rapid scientific and technological development	1	2	3	4	5	6	(23)
(5) Your own increasing maturity	1	2	3	4	5	6	(24)
(6) Study or discussion with peers	1	2	3	4	5	6	(25)
(7) Urbanization and secularization in society	1	2	3	4	5	6	(26)
(8) Personal conversion or very moving experience	1	2	3	4	5	6	(27)
(9) Recent developments in the field of theology	1	2	3	4	5	6	(28)
(10) Irrelevance of ministry to problems of world	1	2	3	4	5	6	(29)
(11) Closer contact with many kinds of people	1	2	3	4	5	6	(30)
(12) Influence of your wife and family	1	2	3	4	5	6	(31)
(13) Formal continuing education	1	2	3	4	5	6	(32)
(14) Others _____	1	2	3	4	5	6	(33)
(15) _____ There were no significant changes.							(34)

31. Which one of the following best describes the urgency of your situation when you moved from your previous position to your present job?   (35)

     (1) _____ Had no choice—could not have stayed in that position any longer

     (2) _____ Could have stayed in that position awhile longer but less than a year

     (3) _____ Could have stayed in that position a year or more but not indefinitely

     (4) _____ Could have stayed indefinitely in that position

32. Was the *urgency* you just described: (36)

     (1) _____ Due chiefly to your own feelings?

     (2) _____ Due chiefly to the pressures of others to get you out?

     (3) _____ Due chiefly to family problems?

     (4) _____ Others _____

33. Have you had illnesses or chronic physical complaints in recent years?   (37)

     _____ (1) Yes (if yes, please describe): _____
                                     _____

     _____ (2) No

34. If you were to leave your present type of ministry, what kind of work would you like to enter?   (38)

PART V

35. From your experience in ministerial work, what suggestions would you like to make to each of the following (use extra pages as needed):
    (1) The congregation (or other religious organization) you serve now?

    (2) Your seminary?

    (3) Fellow pastors?

    (4) Laymen?

    (5) Church administrators (conference, association, national staff)?

36. Are there specific issues you would like to hear discussed among ministers and denominational leaders? If so, please list and describe them.

Truman B. Douglass, Executive Vice President   Howard E. Spragg, Treasurer

UNITED CHURCH BOARD FOR HOMELAND MINISTRIES

28 November 1967 *

Dear _____:

I am writing to ask for the names and addresses of those men in your conference who have withdrawn from the pastoral ministry to earn their living outside religious institutions.

Many of us are alarmed at the increasing numbers of men who are leaving the pastoral ministry. When we begin to examine the problem critically, a paucity of data is at once revealed. We do not know what formal attempts have been made to minister to or listen to these men.

A series of weekend consultations with some of these men are contemplated during the late spring of 1968. We want to understand what they are saying and feeling about the church. We will consider our conversations a means of informing Board policy in such areas as in-service training for ministers. We realize, of course, that other instrumentalities of the United Church are concerned about this problem, and their representatives will be participating in the consultations.

Attached herewith are forms which I hope you will use in reporting. When we have the names in hand, the men will be invited to a regional weekend consultation. In order that you may be kept posted, you will receive a copy of our initial correspondence with the men.

Thank you for your kind attention to this matter.

Sincerely yours,

HOWARD E. SPRAGG
HES:VKS
Enclosure

* Letter sent to conference executives asking for names of ministers who have withdrawn from the pastoral ministry.

March 12, 1968 *

Dear _____ :

We have set our heart and hand to devise a means of disciplined listening to men who have withdrawn from the pastoral ministry to earn their living outside ecclesiastical institutions. The results of this UCC study will have wide distribution and will undoubtedly influence church policy in American Protestantism.

To this end you have been invited to a regional conference nearest you.

Now in order to learn from, it is also necessary to learn about. The enclosed set of questions will fulfill both goals and will help us prepare for these conferences which are to be held in May and June.

We will be much indebted to you if you will complete the questionnaire and return it at your early convenience even if you cannot attend a conference.

Please note the following:

1. We have asked the Department of Research of the National Council of Churches to do both content analysis and computer work relative to the returns. You will note that the return envelope has that address.

2. Although we request your name, you may rest assured that the material will be kept confidential and will not in any way become part of your dossier.

3. All those contributing to the study will receive a report of the results of the study.

4. If you want to write on some subject not raised, please do so. We really want to hear you, and will pay careful attention to the material you send.

If you have not replied to our invitation to participate in a listening conference, we hope that you will do so soon.

Warm regards,

Howard E. Spragg
Dean

Gerald J. Jud
Conference Director

* Letter of invitation to regional conferences, sent to 370 ex-pastors.

INSTRUCTIONS FOR INTERVIEWERS

UCC STUDY OF CLERGY IN SECULAR WORK

The purpose of the interviews is twofold: to give each man an opportunity to tell his story to someone, and to learn as much as possible about the process of leaving church work for secular employment. These interviews are not therapy, they are not an occasion for recruitment back into church work, nor are they gathering of information for a man's dossier. They are part of a study of career decision processes in the ministry. This research is being done through the Department of Ministry and the Department of Research of the National Council of Churches, in cooperation with the Board for Homeland Ministries of the United Church of Christ. It is one aspect of an extensive study of career patterns among clergymen being undertaken by the Department of Ministry. Reports of findings will be available in two forms: Dr. Gerald Jud will be making a report to the United Church of Christ on the conferences and their implications for church policy and practice; later, the research will be reported as a published study by the Department of Ministry.

I. The Interview Situation

The interview guide for this one-hour contact is rather fully structured, partly to ensure the broadest possible coverage of material in such a short time, and partly to standardize the conduct of the interviews by a very diverse group of interviewers. Although you need not try to become a mere function, you should subdue your own personal style and let the questions themselves provide the stimulus value. You should influence as little as possible the content of the respondent's remarks, although admittedly the line between evocation and influence is a fine one.

The interview guide has been structured in three parts, beginning with the present. Detailed instructions about questions and probes are included on the guide. You should be so familiar with the questions and their location that you can move from one place to another inserting answers even when they are given out of order. A number of sensitive issues are probed, including personal faith, marital situation, and handling of conflict. These are exceedingly important for the understanding of career decisions, and you should return to them later if satisfactory answers are not forthcoming the first time.

Prior to the interviews you will be given the advance questionnaires received from your respondents. They should know that you have seen these questionnaires and already have information about them. Early in the conference, in addition to the interview period, respondents will be asked to complete yet another written instrument which is complementary to the interview. They may sometimes feel that they have already answered on paper the questions you are asking, but it is not actually so.

Some suggestions for interviewing:

1. At the beginning take a few moments for informal conversation; inquiries about the respondent's present work or "I used to live in Chicago too" remarks will put you both at ease.

2. Ask the question and wait for the response. Don't be anxious about silences. As you go along, your judgment will improve about whether to recall a voluble person to the question or whether to ask a reticent one, "Is there anything you'd like to add?"

3. Ask the question *as written*, resisting temptations to interpret it. If the respondent asks, "What do you mean?" you should restate the question and add, "Answer it as it is meaningful to you." Do *not* explain or interpret for him.

II. Reporting the Interview

You are dealing with people who have made their living by talking. You will not catch every word on paper, nor will all those words be valuable. Here your decision is critical, since it will influence the research immensely. The rule of thumb is: Get the initial response verbatim if possible, and later portions also if they seem quite important. Signs of importance include: causal statements, strong feelings, time sequences, incidents.

You may occasionally have to say, "That seems quite important—would you wait a moment so I can get it all down?" or even ask him to repeat.

In addition to the completion of the interview, we are asking you to spend ten minutes (or less) dictating your observations immediately following each interview. Equipment will be provided for this purpose. Any number of topics may occur to you for inclusion, but please be sure to mention the following as appropriate:

1. Is there any effect that will not come through on the written report?

2. Are there unspoken matters which you feel could be quite important but which were not shared?

3. Have you any comments on specific points such as conflicts, marital situations, faith crises, or others?

4. On the whole, why in your opinion did this person leave church work?

5. Does this person seem an unusually sensitive or perceptive commentator, such that he might be further engaged as an adviser to the church?

6. Observations on the flow of topics in the interview.

• • •

We are grateful to you for the time and energy you are giving to this study. Our resources are such that it would not be possible without you. We invite your suggestions and comments both about the study and about possible interpretations of the data. As soon as a progress report is ready, we will share it with you. In particular, if after the conferences are over you wish to make your own suggestions about the research or about the significance of the conference to the United Church of Christ, we hope you will do so soon.

Edgar W. Mills

APPENDIX B / TABULATION OF DATA

Table B1. Self-description of Ex-Pastors and Pastors

	EX–PASTORS	
	NUMBER	PERCENT
Have left the ministry	32	13.9
Still in the ministry but have left the pastorate	142	61.5
Only temporarily out of the pastorate	14	6.1
Other (write in)	27	11.7
No response	16	6.9
	231	100.1

	PASTORS	
	NUMBER	PERCENT
Permanently in the pastorate	94	37.6
Permanently in the ministry but not committed to staying in the pastorate	118	47.2
Planning on a specific nonparish ministry	9	3.6
Expecting to enter secular work	3	1.2
Other	24	9.6
No response	2	0.8
	250	100.0

Table B2. Size of Community Lived in During Teen Years

NUMBER OF INHABITANTS	EX–PASTORS		PASTORS	
	NUMBER	PERCENT	NUMBER	PERCENT
Under 2,500 (rural)	61	26.4	71	28.4
2,500–9,999 (town)	36	15.6	45	18.0
10,000–49,999 (small city)	48	20.8	38	15.2
50,000 & over (metropolitan-suburban)	32	13.9	28	11.2
50,000 & over (metropolitan-inner city)	18	7.8	21	8.4
50,000 & over (other metropolitan)	29	12.6	45	18.0
No response	7	3.0	2	0.8
	231	100.1	250	100.0

Table B3. Fathers' Occupations of Ex-Pastors and Pastors

	EX–PASTORS		PASTORS	
	NUMBER	PERCENT	NUMBER	PERCENT
Clergyman	30	13.0	33	13.2
Other professional	28	12.1	23	9.2
Manager, official, or proprietor	37	16.0	32	12.8
Sales worker	9	3.9	7	2.8
Secretarial or clerical worker	10	4.3	12	4.8
Craftsman, foreman, or operative	42	18.2	59	23.6
Farmer or farm manager	28	12.1	47	18.8
Household worker, laborer, service worker	25	10.8	17	6.8
Other or not applicable	18	7.8	19	7.6
No response	4	1.7	1	0.4
	231	99.9	250	100.0

Table B4. Race of Ex-Pastors and Pastors

	EX–PASTORS		PASTORS	
	NUMBER	PERCENT	NUMBER	PERCENT
Black (Negro)	5	2.2	4	1.6
White	221	95.7	238	95.2
Oriental and other	1	0.4	3	1.2
No response	4	1.7	5	2.0
	231	100.0	250	100.0

Table B5. Denomination of First Church Membership

	EX–PASTORS		PASTORS	
	NUMBER	PERCENT	NUMBER	PERCENT
UCC	5	2.2	11	4.4
Congregational Christian	62	26.8	61	24.4
Evangelical & Reformed	33	14.3	82	32.8
Baptist	27	11.7	16	6.4
Lutheran	6	2.6	5	2.0
Presbyterian & Reformed	26	11.3	13	5.2
Methodist & EUB	39	16.9	33	13.2
All others	28	12.1	28	11.2
No response	5	2.2	1	0.4
	231	100.1	250	100.0

Table B6. College Major of Ex-Pastors and Pastors

	EX–PASTORS		PASTORS	
	NUMBER	PERCENT	NUMBER	PERCENT
Natural science & math	18	7.8	9	3.6
Social science	64	27.7	47	18.8
Humanities (including history)	105	45.5	122	48.8
Religion	18	7.8	34	13.6
Engineering & technical	3	1.3	1	0.4
Social work, counseling	0	0	5	2.0
Education	6	2.6	9	3.6
Other or no response	17	7.4	23	9.2
	231	100.1	250	100.0

Table B7. Age at Decision to Enter Ministry

YEARS OLD	EX–PASTORS (231) PERCENT	PASTORS (250) PERCENT
14 or under	3.4	7.2
15–19	33.8	40.4
20–24	41.6	35.6
25–29	12.1	11.6
30 or over	6.9	4.4
No response	2.2	0.8
	100.0	100.0
Median age	20.9 yrs.	20.2 yrs.

Table B8. Age at Ordination

AGE WHEN ORDAINED	EX–PASTORS (231) PERCENT	PASTORS (250) PERCENT
24 or under	22.1	20.0
25–29	50.6	63.2
30–34	16.5	8.4
35 or over	8.6	8.0
No response	2.2	0.4
	100.0	100.0
Median age	28.0 yrs.	27.4 yrs.

Table B9. Seminary Attended by Ex-Pastors and Pastors

	EX–PASTORS		PASTORS	
	NUMBER	PERCENT	NUMBER	PERCENT
Chicago	30	13.0	19	7.6
Eden	19	8.2	47	18.8
Lancaster	14	6.1	22	8.8
Andover Newton	20	8.7	23	9.2
Yale	22	9.5	23	9.2
Other UCC seminaries	71	30.8	63	25.2
Other denominational seminaries	40	17.3	32	12.8
Inter- or nondenominational seminaries	8	3.5	12	4.8
Did not attend seminary	7	3.0	9	3.6
	231	100.1	250	100.0

Table B10. Marital Status of Ex-Pastors and Pastors

	EX–PASTORS		PASTORS	
	NUMBER	PERCENT	NUMBER	PERCENT
Married	189	81.8	230	92.0
Married and now separated	2	0.9	0	0
Divorced	11	4.8	2	0.8
Divorced and remarried	14	6.1	5	2.0
Widowed	0	0	2	0.8
Widowed and remarried	4	1.7	6	2.4
Unmarried	7	3.0	5	2.0
No response	4	1.7	0	0
	231	100.0	250	100.0

Table B11. Number of Children

	EX–PASTORS		PASTORS	
	NUMBER	PERCENT	NUMBER	PERCENT
None	22	9.5	23	9.2
1	23	10.0	29	11.6
2	76	32.9	75	30.0
3	56	24.2	65	26.0
4	42	18.2	41	16.4
5 or more	12	5.2	17	6.8
	231	100.0	250	100.0

Table B12. Education Beyond Seminary

WHERE	EX–PASTORS		PASTORS	
	NUMBER	PERCENT	NUMBER	PERCENT
Theological school	22	9.7	24	9.6
State or city college or university	43	19.0	14	5.6
Private, church-related, or other college or university	42	18.6	15	6.0
Other institutions	7	3.1	6	2.4
None	112	49.5	191	76.4
	226	99.9	250	100.0
HOW MUCH				
Master's degree	70	30.2	35	14.0
Doctorate	22	9.5	12	4.8

Table B13. Major Field of Education Beyond Seminary

	EX–PASTORS		PASTORS	
	NUMBER	PERCENT	NUMBER	PERCENT
Natural science & math	6	2.7	1	0.4
Social science	16	7.1	3	1.2
Humanities (including history)	29	12.8	12	4.8
Religion	28	12.4	34	13.6
Engineering & technical	0	0	0	0
Social work, counseling	19	8.4	4	1.6
Education	10	4.4	4	1.6
Other	8	3.5	6	2.4
None	110	48.6	186	74.4
	226	99.9	250	100.0

Table B14. Years Since Leaving Church Employment

EX–PASTORS			PASTORS		
YEARS SINCE LEAVING	NUMBER	PERCENT	YEARS SINCE LAST MOVE	NUMBER	PERCENT
0	24	10.4	0	4	1.6
1	56	24.2	1	27	10.8
2	37	16.0	2	29	11.6
3	33	14.3	3	40	16.0
4	21	9.1	4	25	10.0
5–9	32	13.8	5–9	74	29.6
10–14	8	3.5	10–14	31	12.4
15 and over	13	5.6	15 and over	20	8.0
No response	7	3.0		250	100.0
	231	99.9			

Median: 2.96 yrs.

Median: 5.0 yrs.

Table B15. Percent of Ex-Pastors and Pastors in Each Age-group

AGE-GROUP	EX-PASTORS WHEN LEFT LAST CHURCH POSITION	PASTORS WHEN LEFT LAST CHURCH POSITION	PASTORS NOW
29 and under	12.1	14.4	3.2
30–34	22.5	24.0	17.6
35–39	19.1	17.6	17.2
40–44	19.5	12.4	16.0
45–49	11.3	9.6	8.8
50–54	8.2	9.2	11.6
55–59	1.7	4.4	10.4
60–64	2.2	3.2	8.0
65 and over	0	1.6	5.6
No response	3.4	3.6	1.6
	100.0	100.0	100.0
Number of persons	231	250	
Median age	38.9 yrs.	38.2 yrs.	43.4 yrs.

Table B16. Percent of Ex-Pastors Reporting Financial Improvement or Loss, at Age of Leaving

AGE AT MOVE	SOME OR MUCH IMPROVEMENT	ABOUT THE SAME	SOME OR MUCH LOSS	TOTAL
30 or under	62.5	16.7	20.8	100.0
31–40	57.4	24.1	18.5	100.0
41–50	55.2	10.3	34.5	100.0
51 or over	47.1	17.6	35.3	100.0
All ages	56.4	18.5	25.0	99.9
Number of persons	124			

Table B17. Last Church Position of Ex-Pastors and Current Position of Pastors

| | EX–PASTORS | | PASTORS | |
POSITION	NUMBER	PERCENT	NUMBER	PERCENT
Pastor	173	74.9	193	77.2
Associate, assistant, or parish staff	36	15.6	15	6.0
Nonparish minister	12	5.2	37	14.8
No response	10	4.3	5	2.0
	231	100.0	250	100.0

Table B18. Number of Positions of a Given Length Reported by Ex-Pastors and Pastors *

| LENGTH OF POSITION (IN YEARS) | EX–PASTORS (231) | | PASTORS (250) | |
	NUMBER	PERCENT	NUMBER	PERCENT
1	198	19.7	83	10.3
2	270	26.9	154	19.1
3	194	19.3	159	19.7
4	146	14.5	108	13.4
5–6	120	12.0	158	19.6
7–8	47	4.7	73	9.0
9–10	15	1.5	32	4.0
11–15	9	0.9	27	3.3
16 and over	5	0.5	14	1.7
	1,004	100.0	808	100.1

* Although this table excludes the post-pastorate secular jobs of ex-pastors, the form of our data made it impossible to exclude from these figures the secular positions occupied by clergy at earlier points in their lives. We assume that ex-pastors' and pastors' secular work patterns are similar to their clergy employment patterns.

Table B19. How Move Affected Ex-Pastors' Financial Circumstances

	NUMBER	PERCENT
Much improvement	39	29.8
Some improvement	33	25.2
About the same	25	19.1
Some loss	15	11.5
Much loss	16	12.2
No response	3	2.3
	131	100.1

Table B20. Comparison of Current and Last Ministerial Salaries of Ex-Pastors

SALARY	CURRENT POSITION		LAST MINISTERIAL POSITION	
	NUMBER	PERCENT	NUMBER	PERCENT
Under $4,000	1	1.2	13	10.7
$4,000–5,999	4	4.9	42	34.7
$6,000–7,999	16	19.5	43	35.5
$8,000–9,999	24	29.3	14	11.6
$10,000–14,999	28	34.1	8	6.6
$15,000 and over	9	11.0	1	0.8
	82	100.0	121	99.9
Median salary	$9,667		$6,256	

Table B21. Comparison of Current Salaries and Earliest Salaries of Ex-Pastors and Pastors

SALARY	EX–PASTORS CURRENT POSITION		PASTORS CURRENT POSITION	
	NUMBER	PERCENT	NUMBER	PERCENT
Under $4,000	1	1.2	6	2.5
$4,000–5,999	4	4.9	36	14.9
$6,000–7,999	16	19.5	73	30.2
$8,000–9,999	24	29.3	67	27.7
$10,000–14,999	28	34.1	55	22.7
$15,000 and over	9	11.0	5	2.1
	82	100.0	242	100.1
Median salary	$9,667		$8,179	

SALARY	EX–PASTORS—FIRST MINISTRY POSITION		PASTORS—FIRST MINISTRY POSITION	
	NUMBER	PERCENT	NUMBER	PERCENT
Under $4,000	68	55.7	125	52.5
$4,000–5,999	36	29.5	79	33.2
$6,000–7,999	14	11.5	27	11.3
$8,000–9,999	1	0.8	4	1.7
$10,000–14,999	2	1.6	2	0.8
$15,000 and over	1	0.8	1	0.4
	122	99.9	238	99.9
Median salary	$3,588		$3,808	

Table B22. Ex-Pastors' Ratings of Importance of Reasons for Leaving Their Last Position

	DEGREE OF IMPORTANCE (percent)			
REASONS	NONE	LOW	MEDIUM	HIGH
1. Inadequate salary or living arrangements	34.4	32.8	22.1	11.7
2. Serious conflict with colleague(s) over job responsibilities or other matters	65.7	13.0	11.5	9.9
3. Opportunity arose to do specialized work or training	45.8	7.6	7.6	38.9
4. Wife or family unhappy	45.8	19.9	17.6	16.8
5. Felt personal inadequacy as church leader	42.8	23.7	14.5	19.1
6. Unable to relocate in ministry when move became necessary	66.4	6.9	11.5	15.3
7. Family would greatly benefit by move	52.7	10.7	18.3	18.3
8. Serious conflict with laymen over how to conduct church affairs	43.5	25.2	16.0	15.3
9. Crisis in personal life made a move necessary	64.1	9.9	10.7	14.3
10. Uncertain of own vocation to ministry	44.3	18.3	16.8	20.6
11. Higher salary or fringe benefits offered	51.2	19.8	15.3	13.7
12. Disillusioned with the church's relevance to problems of modern world	19.9	13.0	23.7	43.5
13. Health problems made a change necessary	81.7	6.1	6.9	5.3
14. Church coerced move by making things "too hot" for you	65.6	10.7	13.0	10.7
15. Opportunity arose for larger ministry with greater responsibility	63.4	6.9	8.4	21.4
16. Change coerced by denominational leadership	82.4	6.9	3.8	6.9
17. Change was a planned step in a long-range career plan	61.8	12.2	12.2	13.7
18. More desirable region or community	79.4	7.6	6.1	6.9
19. Trouble *among* parishioners interfered with your ministry there	61.8	16.0	13.0	9.2
20. To improve that church (or organization) seemed a hopeless task	36.6	26.0	20.6	16.8
21. Your own personal faith changed	60.3	24.4	9.9	5.3
22. Church did not take your leadership seriously	43.5	19.1	27.5	9.9
23. Didn't enjoy the work of the pastorate	35.1	29.8	19.1	16.0
24. Very attractive type of work offered	46.6	9.9	10.7	32.8
Number of persons	131			

Table B23. Money as a Factor in Ex-Pastors' Decisions to Leave

	NUMBER	PERCENT
Money very much a factor in the decision	16	12.2
Money a moderate factor	14	10.7
Money had some part but not much	4	3.1
Money had nothing to do with the decision	76	58.0
Unknown	21	16.0
	131	100.0

Table B24. Conditions Under Which Ex-Pastors Would Have Stayed in Church Employment

I WOULD HAVE STAYED:	NUMBER	PERCENT
If church were different . . .		
—If church had moved toward a new or more relevant ministry	25	19.1
—If either the minister's role or my personality were different	16	12.2
If more appropriate job had appeared . . .		
—If I had gotten a job to fit my interests or abilities	17	13.0
—If I had been able to get a job immediately	17	13.0
—If the job had been more satisfying	8	6.1
—If the offer of another job had *not* come	3	2.3
If the circumstantial pressures on me had been different . . .		
—If I had had more money or better living conditions	10	7.6
—If I had had time to rethink or renew my vocation	6	4.6
—If I had remained married	5	3.8
—If I had not felt compelled to resign	3	2.3
I would not have stayed	8	6.1
Unknown	13	9.9
	131	100.0

Table B25. Ex-Pastors and Pastors Highly Valuing the Praise * of Potential
Reference Persons and Groups During Pastorate

DURING PASTORATE, HIGHLY VALUED PRAISE OF:	EX–PASTORS			PASTORS		
	NUMBER	PERCENT	TOTAL NUMBER	NUMBER	PERCENT	TOTAL NUMBER
Fellow UCC pastors	40	32.0	125	67	28.3	237
Denomination executive who knew your work best	67	55.4	121	106	44.9	236
Lay leaders in congregation	72	57.6	125	151	63.7	237
Wife	91	77.8	117	184	77.6	237
Fellow pastors in churches of same community	36	29.8	121	48	21.0	229
Others on your church staff (if any)	45	48.4	93	75	46.6	161
Close friends not included above	69	58.5	118	124	53.7	231

* "High values" refer to ratings of 5 or 6 on a six-point scale ranging from "not at all" to "extremely much."

Table B26. High Ratings * of Potential Support System Elements During
Pastorate by Ex-Pastors and Pastors

PERSON OR GROUP	PERCENT HIGHLY SUPPORTIVE		PERCENT HIGHLY ISOLATING	
	EX-PASTORS (131)	PASTORS (250)	EX-PASTORS (131)	PASTORS (250)
Fellow UCC pastors	25.4	21.8	16.3	13.3
Denomination executive who knew your work best	35.4	32.8	13.7	8.2
Lay leaders in congregation	42.4	56.3	15.6	8.2
Wife	75.8	85.2	5.9	2.8
Fellow pastors in churches of same community	20.8	21.3	13.0	10.6
Others on your church staff (if any)	50.0	56.8	10.3	2.8
Close friends not included above	59.8	58.0	0.9	1.5

* "High values" refer to ratings of 5 or 6 on a six-point scale ranging from "not at all" to "extremely much."

Table B27. Change in Self-image Since Entering Secular Work

	EX–PASTORS	
	NUMBER	PERCENT
Freer as a person	20	15.3
More confident, more adequate	28	21.4
Generally better	12	9.2
About the same	23	17.5
Not as good, troubled	25	19.1
Not enough data	23	17.5
	131	100.0

Table B28. Family Problems of Ex-Pastors and the Decision to Leave

	NUMBER	PERCENT
Had severe problems which led to divorce or separation	14	10.7
Had severe problems which have become better	13	9.9
Problems were a contributing factor in the decision and are improved since leaving	19	14.5
Problems not a cause but family situation happier now	36	27.5
No change in family situation	26	19.9
Family unhappier now	7	5.3
Unmarried at the time	8	6.1
Other or no response	8	6.1
	131	100.0

Table B29. Why Ministers Went to Seminary

	EX–PASTORS		PASTORS	
	NUMBER	PERCENT	NUMBER	PERCENT
Seeking a *faith*	18	7.8	11	4.4
Already a believer, and seeking a *vocation*	47	20.4	35	14.0
Already clear about vocation and seeking to *prepare* for it	134	58.0	196	78.4
Other	16	6.9	5	2.0
No response	16	6.9	3	1.2
	231	100.0	250	100.0

Table B30. Stress Reported by Pastors in Current Jobs and by Ex-Pastors in Their Last Ministerial Jobs

STRESS RATING * IN WORK	EX–PASTORS—LAST MINISTERIAL JOB		PASTORS— CURRENT JOB	
	NUMBER	PERCENT	NUMBER	PERCENT
High	42	33.3	55	22.0
Medium	51	40.5	100	40.0
Low	29	23.0	75	30.0
No response	4	3.2	20	8.0
	126	100.0	250	100.0

* Recorded on a six-point scale from "least or no stress" (1) to "most stress" (6) personally felt by respondent in that position. High stress means ratings of 5 or 6, medium means ratings of 3 or 4, and low means ratings of 1 or 2.

BIBLIOGRAPHY

BIBLIOGRAPHY

Clergy and Church

Bentz, W. Kenneth. "Consensus Between Role Expectations and Role Behavior Among Ministers," *Community Mental Health Journal,* IV, 4 (1968), 301–6.

Berg, Philip L. "Mangled or Molded: A Survey of Seminarians," *United Church Herald,* XI, 11 (1968), 7m.

Blizzard, Samuel W. "The Minister's Dilemma," *The Christian Century,* LXXIII, 17 (1956), 508–10.

———. "The Parish Minister's Integrating Roles," *Religious Education,* LIII, 4 (1958), 374–80.

———. "The Parish Minister's Self-Image of His Master Role," *Pastoral Psychology,* IX, 89 (1958–59), 25.

Bowers, Margaretta K. *Conflicts of the Clergy.* New York: Thomas Nelson & Sons, 1963.

Braude, Lee. "Professional Autonomy and the Role of the Layman," *Social Forces,* XXXIV, 4 (1960), 297.

Burch, Genevieve. "Career Change of Clergy to Secular Occupations: Development of a Theoretical Framework." Unpublished M.A. Thesis, University of Maryland, 1969.

Cavert, Samuel McCrea. "The Minister's Distinctive Role," *Pastoral Psychology,* XI, 101 (1960–61), 16.

Centers, Richard. "Attitudes and Belief in Relation to Occupational Stratification," *Journal of Social Psychology,* XXVII, 2 (1948), 159–85.

Chapman, Stanley H. "The Minister: Professional Man of the Church," *Social Forces,* XXIII, 2 (1945), 202–6.

The Church for Others and the Church for the World: A Quest for Structures for Missionary Congregations, Final Report of the Western European Working Group and North American Working Group of the Department on Studies in Evangelism (Geneva, Switzerland: World Council of Churches, 1967).

Declan, Peter. "Trial by Laicization," *Commonweal,* LXXXV, 10 (1967), 328–31.

Dittes, James E. "Research on Clergymen: Factors Influencing Decisions for Religious Service and Effectiveness in the Vocation," *Review of Recent Research Bearing on Religious and Character Education*. Published as a supplement to *Religious Education* (July–August 1962). New York: Religious Education Association, 1962.

Douglass, H. Paul, and Brunner, Edmund. *The Protestant Church as a Social Institution*. New York: Harper & Brothers, 1935.

Fichter, Joseph. "Clergy," in *Professionalization,* ed. Howard M. Vollmer and Donald L. Mills. Englewood Cliffs, New Jersey: Prentice-Hall, 1966. Pp. 145–67.

————. *Religion as an Occupation*. South Bend: University of Notre Dame Press, 1966.

————. *America's Forgotten Priests: What They Are Saying*. New York: Harper & Row, 1968.

Glock, Charles Y., and Ringer, Benjamin. "Church Policy and the Attitudes of Ministers and Parishioners on Social Issues," *American Sociological Review,* XXI, 2 (1956), 148–56.

Glock, Charles Y., and Roos, Phillip. "Parishioners' Views of How Ministers Spend Their Time," *Review of Religious Research,* II, 4 (1960–61), 170–77.

Gustafson, James M. "An Analysis of the Problem of the Role of the Minister," *Journal of Religion,* XXXIV, 3 (1954), 187–91.

————. "The Clergy in the United States," *Daedalus,* XCII, 2 (Fall 1963), 724–44.

————. "The Clergy in the United States," *The Professions in America,* ed. Kenneth S. Lynn. New York: Houghton Mifflin Co., 1963.

Hadden, Jeffrey K. *The Gathering Storm in the Churches*. New York: Doubleday, 1969.

Hall, Douglas T., and Schneider, Benjamin. "A Study of Work Experiences and Career Growth of Roman Catholic Diocesan Priests." New Haven, Connecticut: Yale University, Department of Administrative Sciences, March 1969.

Higgins, Paul S., and Dittes, James E. "Change in Laymen's Expectations of the Minister's Role," *Ministry Studies,* II, 1 (1968), 5–8.

Kennedy, Eugene C., M.M. "Psychological Consequences," in Mills, ed., "Role Conflict Among Clergy," *Ministry Studies,* II, 3–4 (December 1968), 50–51.

McCune, S. D., and Mills, Edgar W. "An Evaluation of Continuing Education for Ministers." Washington: Ministry Studies Board, 1968.

MacLeod, Jack M. "Are Ministers in Short Supply?" *Monday Morning.* Indiana: General Council of the United Presbyterian Church in the United States of America, 1969, 11 ff.

Menges, Robert J. "Studies of Clergymen: Abstracts of Research, Supplement 1," *Ministry Studies,* I, 3 (October 1967).

Menges, Robert J., and Dittes, James E. *Psychological Studies of Clergymen: Abstracts of Research*. New York: Thomas Nelson & Sons, 1965.

Merton, Robert K. "Role-Set: Problems in Sociological Theory," *British Journal of Sociology,* VIII (1957), 106 ff.

Mills, Edgar W. "Career Changes Among Ministers," *Harvard Studies in Career Development,* No. 46. Unpublished Ph.D. dissertation, Center for Research in Careers, Cambridge: Harvard University, May 1966.

————. "Career Change in the Protestant Ministry," *Ministry Studies,* III, 1 (May 1969).

Moberg, David O. *The Church as a Social Institution.* Englewood Cliffs, New Jersey: Prentice-Hall, 1962.

Pugh, Thomas J. "A Comparative Study of the Values of a Group of Ministers and Two Groups of Laymen," *Journal of Social Psychology,* XXXIII, 2 (1951), 225–35.

Pusey, Nathan M., and Taylor, Charles L. *Ministry for Tomorrow.* New York: Seabury Press, 1967.

Scherer, Ross P. "The Lutheran Ministry: Origins, Careers, Self-Appraisal," *Information Service,* XLII (April 27, 1963), 1–8.

————. "Income and Business Costs of the Protestant Clergy in 1963: A Preliminary Report of a National Council of Churches' Survey of Clergy Support," *Information Service,* XLIII, 19 (December 5, 1964), 1–8.

Skirvin, Sidney D. "Analysis of the Third 'Withdrawal' Conference of the UCC," Union Theological Seminary (New York), 1968, mimeographed, 9 pp.

Smith, James O., and Sjoberg, Gideon. "Origins and Career Patterns of Leading Protestant Clergymen," *Social Forces,* XXXIX, 3 (1960), 290–96.

Smith, Luke M. "The Clergy: Authority Structure, Ideology, Migration," *American Sociological Review,* XVIII, 3 (1953), 242–48.

Spangenberg, James L. "A Theoretical Model for Role Cluster Analysis Tested with Thirty Ministers' Families." Unpublished Ph.D. dissertation, Pennsylvania State University, 1966.

Strunk, Otto. "Men, Motives and the Ministry," *Religious Education,* LIV, 5 (1959), 429–34.

Thornton, Edward E. "Ministerial Drop-Outs: A Note," *Journal of Pastoral Care,* XIV, 1 (1960), 118.

Troeltsch, Ernst. "The Emergence of Types of Religious Organizations," in *Reader on Bureaucracy,* ed. Robert Merton. New York: Free Press of Glencoe, 1952. Pp. 79–85.

U.S. Department of H.E.W., Public Health Service. *Bibliography on Religion and Mental Health, 1960–1964.* Washington, D.C.: U.S. Government Printing Office, 1967.

Werner, Ernest. "Remodeling the Protestant Ministry," *American Scholar,* XXXIV, 1 (1966), 31–49.

Whitlock, Glenn E. "Role and Self-Concepts in the Choice of the Ministry as a Vocation," *Journal of Pastoral Care,* XVII, 4 (1963), 208–12.

Winter, J. Alan, and Mills, Edgar W. "Research on Training for Metropolitan Ministry, Reports 203, 208, 209." Washington, D.C.: Ministry Studies Board, 1969, mimeographed.

Young, J. H. Wallace. "A Profile of Those Who Leave," *Tomorrow* (May 1969), 6–11.

190

Other Relevant Works

Barber, Bernard. "Some Problems in the Sociology of the Professions," in *The Professions in America,* ed. Kenneth S. Lynn. New York: Houghton Mifflin Co., 1963. Pp. 18–20.

Blalock, Hubert M. *Social Statistics.* New York: McGraw-Hill, 1960.

Blau, Peter. *Exchange and Power in Social Life.* New York: John Wiley & Sons, 1957.

Caplow, Theodore. "General Look at Occupational Images and Norms," in *Professionalization,* ed. Howard M. Vollmer and Donald L. Mills. Englewood Cliffs, New Jersey: Prentice-Hall, 1966. Pp. 113–14.

Carrier, Herve, and Pin, Emile. *Sociology of Christianity, International Bibliography.* Rome: Georgian University Press, 1964.

Etzioni, Amitai. "Two Approaches to Organizational Analysis," *Administrative Science Quarterly,* V, 2 (1960), 257–78.

―――. *A Comparative Analysis of Complex Organizations.* Glencoe, Illinois: The Free Press, 1961.

Friedmann, E. A., and Havighurst, R. J. "Work and Retirement," in *Man, Work and Society,* ed. Sigmund Nosow and William H. Form. New York: Basic Books Inc., 1962. Pp. 41–55.

Georgopoulos, Basil S., and Tannenbaum, Arnold S. "A Study of Organizational Effectiveness," *American Sociological Review,* XXII, 5 (1957), 534–40.

Glaser, Barney G. *Organizational Careers: A Sourcebook for Theory.* Chicago: Aldine Publishing Co., 1968.

Glock, Charles Y. "The Sociology of Religion," in *Sociology Today,* ed. Robert K. Merton. New York: Basic Books Inc., 1962. Pp. 153–70.

Gouldner, Alvin. "Reciprocity and Autonomy in Functional Theory," in *Symposium on Sociological Theory,* ed. L. Gross. New York: Harper and Brothers, 1959. Pp. 241–70.

―――. "The Norms of Reciprocity: A Preliminary Statement," *American Sociological Review,* XXV, 2 (1960), 161–78.

―――. "Organizational Analysis," in *Sociology Today,* ed. Robert K. Merton, et al. New York: Basic Books Inc., 1962. Pp. 400–428.

Hilton, Thomas, et al. "Cognitive Processes in Career Decision-making," Cooperative Research Project No. 1046. Pittsburgh: Carnegie Institute of Technology, 1962.

Hughes, Everett C. *Men and Their Work.* New York: Free Press of Glencoe, 1958.

March, James, and Simon, Herbert. *Organizations.* New York: John Wiley and Sons, 1958.

Merton, Robert K.; Reader, George; and Kendall, Patricia; eds. *The Student-Physician: Introductory Studies in the Sociology of Medical Education.* Cambridge: Harvard University Press, 1957.

Roe, Anne. *Psychology of Occupations.* New York: Wiley and Sons, 1956.

Roe, Anne, and Baruch, Rhoda. "Factors Influencing Occupational Decisions,"

Center for Research in Careers, *Harvard Career Studies,* No. 32. Cambridge: Harvard University, 1964.

Selltitz, Clare; Jahoda, Marie; Deutsch, Morton; and Cook, Stuart. *Research Methods in Social Relations.* New York: Holt, Rinehart & Winston, 1962.

Sherif, M., and Wilson, M. O. *Group Relations at the Crossroads.* New York: Harper and Brothers, 1953.

Shibutani, Tamotsu. "Reference Groups and Social Control," in *Human Behavior and Social Processes,* ed. Arnold Rose. Boston: Houghton Mifflin Co., 1962.

Slocum, Walter. *Occupational Careers.* Chicago: Aldine Publishing Co., 1966.

Strauss, Anselm, and Rainwater, Lee. *The Professional Scientist.* Chicago: Aldine Publishing Co., 1962.

Super, Donald E. *Psychology of Careers.* New York: Harper and Brothers, 1957.

―――, et al. *Career Development: Self-Concept Theory.* Research Monograph No. 4. New York: College Entrance Examination Board, 1963.

―――. "A Theory of Vocational Development," in *Vocational Guidance and Career Development,* ed. Herman J. Peters and James C. Hansen. New York: Macmillan, 1966. Pp. 99–109.

Vollmer, Howard M., and Mills, Donald L., eds. *Professionalization.* Englewood Cliffs, New Jersey: Prentice-Hall, 1966.

Vroom, Victor H. *Work and Motivation.* New York: John Wiley and Sons, 1964.

Wilensky, Harold. "The Professionalization of Everyone," *American Journal of Sociology,* LXX, 2 (1965), 137–58.